From the author of
The Ultimate Pipe Book

PIPESMOKING
A 21ST CENTURY GUIDE

by

Richard Carleton Hacker

Autumngold Publishing™

Beverly Hills, California 90213

First Edition

Other Books by the Same Author

The Ultimate Pipe Book (U.S. Edition)
The Ultimate Pipe Book (British Edition)
Die Kunst Pfeife zu rauchen (German Edition)
Das Handbuch Des Pfeifenrauchers (German Edition)
Rare Smoke — The Ultimate Guide To Pipe Collecting
The Ultimate Cigar Book
Die Welt der Zigarre (German Edition)
The Christmas Pipe
The Muzzleloading Hunter

Videos

The Ultimate Pipe Video (Premiere Edition)
The Ultimate Pipe Video (Collector's Edition)

Audio Tapes

CigarQuest — Conversations In Smoke

Printed in the United States of America.
Library of Congress Control Number: 00-91961
ISBN No. 0-931253-13-6

To my wife, beautiful, charming, infinitely patient and aptly christened "Saint Joan" by those who know her, for having shared all these years with me and my pipes.

TABLE OF CONTENTS

A Brief Introduction by the Author i

Chapter 1
Pipemaking — A Centuries-Old Craft 1

Chapter 2
Picking A Pipe 37

Chapter 3
The Pipesmoking Ritual 73

Chapter 4
Pipe Tobacco — A Never-Ending Quest 105

Chapter 5
Tobacco Taster's Menu Of Blends 133

Chapter 6
The Pipesmoker's Sourcebook 159

"One cannot get any closer to the gentle art of smoking. Richard Carleton Hacker has explored every conceivable aspect of our craft and has enabled all serious pipe smokers in the world to gain knowledge of smoking history as well as current innovations. I thank him for his tremendous contribution; long may it continue."

– Richard Dunhill, Chairman
Alfred Dunhill Ltd.

A BRIEF INTRODUCTION
BY THE AUTHOR

Welcome to the New Age of Pipesmoking. Although it may seem strange to be referring to something that has been around for more than 500 years as "new," that is part of the secret to the pipe's immortality. Throughout the centuries, it is constantly being rediscovered. Puffing smoke from a hollowed device filled with tobacco was first recorded by the Mayans sometime around 500 A.D. in Chiapas, Mexico, but it is a pretty safe bet that pipesmoking was going on long before that. As far as Europe and the New World are concerned, however, pipesmoking got a jump start in popularity in 1586, when Ralph Lane, the first governor of Virginia, returned to England with some interesting souvenirs from the American colonies: an Indian calumet and some tobacco. Lane caused a bit of a media event when he publicly "drank smoke" in the streets of London. Like a magician with a new trick, he soon was demonstrating the pleasures of the pipe to others, most notably Sir Walter Raleigh, who was a favorite of the court. With Queen Elizabeth on his side, Raleigh literally made pipesmoking the hottest new trend in England, and eventually, all of Europe. The rest, as they say, is pipesmoking history.

Through the succeeding centuries, in spite of all the ignorance and prejudice against so innocent and humble an object, the pipe has continued to remain with us, like a loyal friend, unwilling to leave. There are times when it has been in vogue, such as during the 1950s, when fears of the Atomic Age called upon the imagery of a pipe to make us feel safe and secure. Indeed, it seemed as if every magazine ad featured an outdoorsman or a father figure smoking a pipe. Then there was the sexual revolution of the sixties and the *bon vivant* image of the smoking jacket and pipe. Today, the lure of the pipe is twofold. First, it is an economical way to partake of pure tobacco; once you make your initial purchase of a decent pipe, it is a relatively inexpensive matter to keep it smoking. Second, the pipe is resuming its stature as a sophisticated symbol of our culture, like a personal home theater or an ultra-premium

i

whiskey. No longer tethered by tweed-coated imagery, the pipe has emerged as an icon of individuality and the freedom to enjoy life as it is meant to be lived.

Unlike those who speak against it, a pipe has no prejudice. Both common men and uncommon ones are judged as equals by the noble briar. Workers, executives, students and teachers as well as authors, scientists, statesmen, kings, queens and presidents have all been ardent aficionados of the pipe. In fact, the world would be a far better place if all its leaders were pipesmokers.

Although a solid object, the pipe imparts an intangible mental stimulation and relaxation. Pick it up and feel the warmth of the briar, taste the flavorful tobacco, and gaze at the restful wreaths of smoke gracefully rising and dispersing into the air. Then you'll know why the pipe has endured.

My previous book, *The Ultimate Pipe Book*, turned the spotlight on pipesmoking during the last two decades of the 20th century. But the book that you now hold in your hands, *Pipesmoking — A 21st Century Guide*, is the first pipe book to be published for the new millennium, and sets the stage for what lies ahead. It was written specifically for the pipesmoker of today. In many ways, he is the same as the millions of pipesmokers who have come before him. And yet there are differences. Today's pipesmoker is far better educated, much more urbane, and is extremely selective about the pipes he buys and the tobaccos he smokes. Moreover, we are now living in the Age of Information; never before has there been a greater ability to know so much about so little. Unfortunately, there are no fact-checkers on the internet. Consequently, there must be a way to preserve the priceless information about pipesmoking and the timelessness of its heritage. That is why this book was written.

Misunderstood by those who don't know it, being buffeted by the ever-changing winds of acceptance and prejudice, the pipe remains steadily on course as one of mankind's most trusted and loyal companions. So light up and let's set sail for the pages ahead. Welcome aboard!

Happy smoking,

Richard Carleton Hacker

Chapter I

PIPEMAKING –
A CENTURIES-OLD
CRAFT

Although technology has dramatically improved most methods of manufacturing in this digital age, the basic premise of pipemaking has not changed in more than one hundred years. In fact, the primary design and function of a pipe has not changed in over 400 years! All pipes, no matter what their price range, involve some degree of hand labor. The more handwork involved, the more expensive a pipe becomes. As our world becomes more automated, it is rather refreshing to realize that pipes are one of the few remaining items in which the manufacturing process can never become fully automated.

A young William Ashton Taylor carefully inspects aged blocks of briar he has purchased for his Ashton pipemaking operation.

Ever since the 1850s, briar has been the most popular of all pipemaking materials. It is a wood that combines beauty, durability, and individuality with exceptional smoking qualities. Therefore, this is the pipemaking substance that we shall discusss first. Most briar for today's pipes comes from Italy, France, Greece, Corsica and Spain. Albania and Algeria at one time were legendary sources for premium briar, but international situations now make these areas impractical for briar harvesting, if not downright dangerous. Briar also exists in other countries, but it has not proven to be the best quality for pipemaking.

As to the characteristics of the various types of briar used in today's pipes, Spanish Moroccan briar is the softest and consequently, the easiest to carve into a pipe. Grecian briar, which became extremely popular in the 1960s for making finely figured Danish freehands, is the hardest of all. Today, many custom high grades are carved from Corsican briar, which is just as finely figured as the Grecian wood but isn't quite as dense. In fact, during the war years of the early 1940s when briar was difficult to get, Corsican was being used right alongside Algerian briar, as it was very similar in many of its characteristics, specifically density and grain. Ever since the 1960s, Italian briar from Tuscany and Calabria has been used for a great many pipes and today these woods are enjoying increased popularity.

No matter where it is grown, all briar comes from one source, the heath tree — known as *erica arborea* if you want to get scientific — a scrawny bush ranging from 15 to 25 feet in height and normally found along the rugged, rocky coast of the Mediterranean. However, it is not the tree itself that is used for pipemaking, but rather the hardened briar burl that is formed beneath the tree and encased within the root system. It is this briar burl that is harvested, cured (dried), then cut into sections or blocks called *ebauchons*, which will eventually be made into a pipe. If the briar is harvested carefully, the heath tree may live to grow another burl. However, many briar merchants do not take the time or have the skill to conserve this valuable resource, and so sadly, an entire tree is killed for its burl. This practice, if allowed to continue, may eventually put our future briar supply in jeopardy.

It takes a briar burl a minimum of fifteen years to mature to a sufficient pipemaking quality, but the best and consequently the most desirable pipes are made from wood that is substantially much older. This, of course, usually translates into higher costs but infinitely better smoking characteristics.

Why is the age of the wood so important to a pipe? The answer becomes evident when we realize that briar has no annual rings. Instead, it has a grain pattern to show how tumultuous a life it has had. The longer the burl remains in the ground, subjected to the hot, dry, windy environment of the Mediterranean coast, the denser and more pronounced its grain becomes. It is this subsequent grain pattern that enables a briar pipe to breathe, in addition to giving it a distinctive visual character. This combination of wood density, porosity and grain pattern makes aged briar extremely desirable for the pipemaker and immensely enjoyable for the pipesmoker. Of course, an obvious question is, why don't we just make pipes out of the oldest wood obtainable, in order to get the best possible pipes? Cost and availability are the culprits here.

As an example, before World War II, it was possible to purchase a high grade, top quality pipe that was often made from 250-year-old briar. As pipesmoking grew in popularity and more of the older wood that was easily accessible was used up, high-grade pipes began being made from 100-year-old briar, which were still exceptional pieces of wood. However, over the years, briar costs have been increasing and the supply of ancient wood, although still available, has become more difficult to get. By 1984, when my first edition of *The Ultimate Pipe Book* was published in America, the very best mass-produced smoking pipes were normally made from briar that was from 50 to 75 years old. By 1989 most of the more popular pipes were being made from briar that was 25 years old. Today, many mass-market pipemakers are actually boasting of using 15-year-old briar! (Of course, there are limited production and special edition pipes that are still made from briar that has been in the ground for a century or more). Only the cheapest "drugstore pipe" (a common term for any low-quality inexpensive pipe, usually found with a lacquered finish to hide its flaws) is made from briar that is less than 15 years old. Yet at one time, even these low-grade pipes were turned from fifty-year-old wood. Let's face it, a pipe made with 15-year-old briar cannot smoke as well as a pipe made of 25-year-old briar, which in turn cannot equal a pipe made from a 100-year-old burl. The reason is, it takes time for Mother Nature to perfect porosity and graining.

Today, the number of pipesmokers and the demand for high-grade pipes continues to grow far beyond the natural ability of the briar bush to produce burls of suitable density and grain for pipemaking. The briar situation is further compounded by the fact that it is increasingly difficult to find workers who are willing to crawl along the hot, precarious and often inaccessible rocks just to dig for dirty clumps of wood. More money and less danger can be had in a clean, air conditioned office working with computers. In addition, like any plant, briar is continuously subject to the ravages of nature, such as forest fires and insect damage, not to mention the inadvertent destruction of the heath tree itself by the overzealous actions of the harvesters. Yet, as today's pipesmokers become more sophisticated, they are demanding higher-grade wood for their pipes. All of this places an increasingly heavy drain upon a product that is not easily replaceable. After all, no matter how far man has advanced technologically — being able to clone a sheep and land a spaceship on Mars — it still takes nature 250 years to produce a 250-year-old piece of briar. And the older and finer-figured the briar, the more it will cost the pipemaker. Consequently, the more it will cost the pipesmoker.

Basically, there are two styles of grain patterns found on a high-grade pipe: 1) a straight grain, in which there are natural dark, thin lines running vertically on the pipe bowl, and 2) burl or bird's eye, appearing as close knit swirls that are actually the ends of a straight grain. We will go into greater detail on these when discussing what to look for in a pipe (Chapter 2).

Briar is classified into grades, which are often marketed to the consumer in the simplest terms as "firsts" and "seconds." It is the desire of many pipesmokers to have a "first," a perfectly flawless full-grained pipe that exhibits absolutely no imperfections in the wood. Often, the pipemakers refer to these as having "clean" bowls. In other words, they are absolutely perfect, or as perfect as so untamed a force as nature can produce. These pipes always command premium prices, as they offer an added value to the rarity and beauty of the briar. It should be remembered that the pattern of the grain does not affect the smoking qualities of a pipe; it is purely cosmetic, which is why a medium-priced briar may smoke just as well as a high grade costing hundreds of dollars more (as long as both pipes are made from a piece of briar that has been properly treated and carved) and the bowl has total — but not necessarily symmetrical — grain coverage.

A pipe with a sand pit, grain disruption, or other minor visual imperfection is referred to as a "second," and can represent a tremendous bargain for the knowledgeable pipesmoker, as we shall discover in the next chapter. It should be pointed out that in this book I am using the classification of a "first" in the purest pipemaking sense of the term. Anything with a flaw in it, no matter how minor, is a "second" and a pipe with so many imperfections that it must be physically doctored up with synthetic putty "fills" is a "third," a pipe which I consider barely suitable for smoking, unless you like to smoke putty (or mastic, as the pipe trade refers to this patching material) instead of briar. I mention all this because there is a growing trend in the pipemaking industry, due to the increasing difficulty in obtaining fine quality briar, to call a superbly-figured straight grain pipe a "first" even if it has a minor sandpit. Thus, this nomenclature that has been traditionally reserved for a flawless piece of briar is now being redefined to refer only to superior briar density and grain pattern, and not visual or aesthetic purity. In that case, what shall we call a *flawless* first. . . a "first-first?" Moreover, there are still some pipe firms, such as Alfred Dunhill Ltd., which simply *do not* produce seconds; any pipe found on their workbenches with an imperfection,

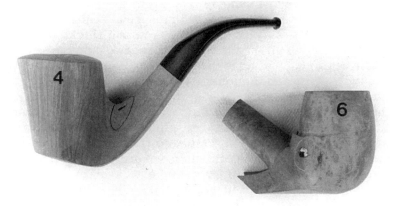

Although a piece of briar may look good from the outside, there may be hidden flaws that can turn up along any of the many pipemaking steps. This is one of the biggest reasons trying to create a perfect pipe can be so frustrating and yet so rewarding.

no matter how trivial, is turned over to another factory and becomes a different pipe brand.

It is important to realize that if you want to smoke a true "first-first" that boasts superb graining and aged, flawless wood, you will have to pay for the privilege, whereas if you smoke a high-grade "second-first" that offers superb wood but may exhibit one or two tiny visual flaws, you must still pay for the privilege, but it won't be quite so high a price. "Seconds" without putty fills are more affordable and for many individuals, are just as aesthetically pleasing. To fully appreciate the basic differences between "firsts" and "seconds," we need to understand the entire pipemaking process, which starts with knowing how the briar gets from the ground to the pipemaker's bench.

Briar is traditionally harvested from November through late Spring. Once the burl has been extracted from the base of the heath tree, it is cleaned by hand and visually inspected for areas that may have been affected by rot and bug damage. These useless pieces of waste are trimmed away. As a result, very often only a 10- to 15-pound-chunk of potentially usable briar is all that is left from a single burl. As soon as each worker has dug out enough briar to constitute a manageable load, he hauls his harvest to a pre-arranged gathering spot. There the burls are kept moist and covered with wet burlap to prevent them from cracking until they can be boiled in water to remove dirt and sap. Then they are shipped to one of the many sawmills in the area that specialize in cutting the briar chunks into *ebauchons*, which are thick, roughly shaped slices of briar from which one or two pipes will eventually be carved. Adding to the cost of the briar is the fact that sawing out the *ebauchons* also produces a great deal of waste. It is during this sawing process that many hidden flaws are discovered within the wood, a reoccurring malady that will continue to plague every pipemaker — from an army of workers in the largest factory to the individual custom craftsman at his home workbench — until the pipe is finally finished. Tiny grains of sand, worm holes, a disruption of the burl's grain, a split in the wood itself — in short, anything that can visually mar the appearance of a completed pipe, often lurks hidden beneath the surface of the wood like some mischievous gremlin, waiting for the chance to jump into view during some stage of the pipe's creation, whether it be in the cutting, carving or sanding processes prior to the pipe's completion. Imagine the frustration of a pipemaker, upon creating a perfectly flawless straight-grained "first," as he gives his prize one final sanding and a sandpit suddenly appears on the bowl. Now he has a "second." That is one of the reasons why firsts are so desirable and costly.

The briar *ebauchons* are then graded according to wood color, grain pattern and size. Usually the darker the wood, the older the briar, and the closer the grain and the larger the piece, the more expensive the *ebauchon* will be. Once it has been categorized, the briar is "cured," which is just another term for aging and drying the wood, a process that takes anywhere from three months to five years, depending upon the quality of the wood and the criteria of the manufacturer. During this aging process, the briar is kept in ventilated sheds and periodically moistened to keep it from cracking.

Years ago, briar was cured naturally by letting it sit in the sun for two or three summers, and wetting it occasionally. In this way, all of the remaining saps and resins were eventually disseminated from the wood. Today, some briar merchants use mechanical sprinklers to keep the briar moist and have devised ways to artificially speed up the drying process. Although I am an advocate of doing things the old way, I should mention that many quality pipemakers employ some of these newer techniques and even though I smoke pipes that have been made by using both the old and the new curing processes, I find there is absolutely no difference in the smoking qualities of a high-grade pipe made in the 1990s as compared to one made in the 1930s. The secret lies in having an aged piece of briar to start with, properly drying it (no matter what the length of time may actually be) and then using the utmost skill and care in creating the pipe. As further proof of this statement, I can point out that pipemaker Mauro Armellini still dries his briar naturally, leaving it stacked up against the sunny side of his house in Italy over a period of seasons. Conversely, Erik Nørding, who makes some of the finest quality high grades to come out of Denmark, invented his own drying machine which he uses to artificially cure all of his wood. Both of these craftsmen produce pipes that are superb smoking instruments, and which are eagerly sought after by experienced smokers. The irony is that Armellini, with his old-fashioned curing process, uses modern machinery to make many of his pipes while Nørding, with his modern briar heating vats, literally hand carves his high-grade pipes in the Old World tradition. Such is the paradox of pipemaking.

The Seven Simplified Steps Of Pipemaking

First the briar *ebauchon* is rough-cut and bored with two holes: the tobacco chamber and a connecting airhole through the stem. It is important that the airhole meets the tobacco chamber at the very bottom of the heel, so that all of the tobacco can be smoked.

The basic shape of the pipe is visualized, either by eye or by drawing a shape, according to the grain of the wood.

Using a saw, the briar is trimmed of excess wood to create the basic shape. Note the rough outline of the tobacco chamber and the use of a pipe cleaner to determine that the airhole has been drilled correctly.

A lathe is usually used to turn the bowl and shank. Otherwise, the final shaping must be done by hand, a much more tedious process.

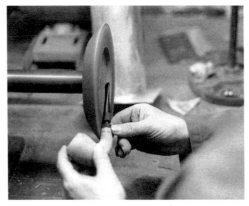

Fitting the stem to the shank can be done by hand with a file or on a finishing wheel. In either case, it is important that the bit fits flush to the shank, so that both pieces flow into each other and conform with the pipe's overall design.

Using gradually finer grits of sandpaper (sometimes as fine as #600 for the final stages), the pipe's surface is gradually smoothed of all finishing marks. Some craftsman try to create an almost glass-like smoothness.

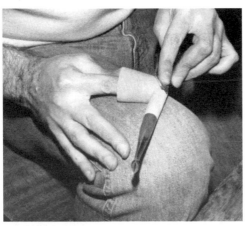

Finally, the pipe is stained, buffed on a wheel, and given a coat of wax to complete the pipemaking process.

No matter how they are dried, once fully cured, the *ebauchons* are again inspected and wood that has cracked or otherwise failed the curing process is discarded, further diminishing the total briar supply. On average, it takes the burls from fifty different heath trees just to find a single flawless piece of briar suitable for a high-grade "first." Finally, the *ebauchons* are sorted into groups and are given letter and numeric designations according to their quality and size. The lowest briar designation is Standard, which is used for pipes that are filled with putty, lacquered to hide their flaws or covered with leather or fur, which may make them visually attractive to the uneducated and totally unsmokable for everyone. Next in grading comes Premium, then Extra and finally Double Extra Quality. Most pipes on today's market are made from Premium Quality wood, which usually yields two or three "firsts" per thousand pipes. The best (and most costly) of the high grades come from Extra Quality plateau briar, the plateau being the outermost — and therefore the hardest — portion of the burl; it is the "choice cut" of briar, usually exhibiting the most dramatic grain and is normally only found on older pieces of wood. Very often a pipemaker will leave plateau briar's rough textured outside surface visible on the top bowl rim of a completed pipe, just to show that it is indeed plateau briar. These Extra Quality plateau *ebauchons* are specially hand picked and assembled in relatively small groups at substantially higher prices than the other *ebauchons*. Not surprisingly, they are often sold individually, rather than in groups.

There is another category of briar, one that is especially desirable not only to premium pipemakers and smokers, but to collectors of "estate pipes," that uniquely American hobby of collecting 20th century pipes that are no longer made. It is known as "dead root." As we now know, the older a burl becomes, the greater its grain pattern and smoking qualities. At some point in its existence, the heath tree and its burl dies. At that point, the burl begins to dry up, in effect curing itself naturally, thereby helping to supplant the man-made process. This is known as "dead root," one of the most sought after and most expensive of all burls. As an example, Alfred Dunhill pipes used to have a designation for their very best high-grade straight grains called DR, which stood for "dead root" and these pipes are highly valued among estate pipe collectors. Even today, many custom pipemakers take great pride if they are able to use dead root briar, and their pipes are priced accordingly. Most briar today is not dead root, which is why it must be artificially cured.

Usually a pipemaker dedicated to only producing high grades will be able to obtain half as many pieces of briar for about twice the price. Often, interested buyers will blanch off a tiny slice of briar from the plateau to try and get an indication of what aesthetic treasures the wood may hold within, but this is a rather nebulous practice, as only by actually carving the pipe can you determine what it will finally look like. Of course, not everyone is intent upon buying only high-grade wood and there are many companies who make nothing but seconds, and pay for their briar accordingly.

Finally, a given number of *ebauchons*, grouped together by grade and size, are placed in burlap bags and sold to buyers of the various pipemaking companies around the world, most notably in England, Denmark, Italy and France. These "briar brokers" are something of a very select secret society. There are not many of them and for the most part, they wish to remain anonymous, as they either have all of the customers that they need or there just simply isn't enough of the high-end plateau briar to go around. It is also for this latter reason that most high-end pipemakers who have a limited production would prefer not to divulge their briar sources.

In determining how much briar to buy, the larger pipemakers, such as Peterson, Stanwell, Savinelli, and Butz-Choquin, for example, buy enough briar to insure that they will have a better chance of creating a profitable supply of "firsts" over a year's time. However, for many of the smaller companies and individual custom pipe carvers, premium prices must be paid for premium briar, and there is never a guarantee that a perfect "first" will be in the batch. I used to wonder why a pipemaker simply did not X-ray his *ebauchons* to determine what secrets the wood contained before he started carving, but I have since been told by more than one pipemaker that good briar has now become so expensive, the realities of the business dictate that they simply buy the wood and take their chances; most can ill-afford to let a single usable piece slip by unfulfilled towards its final destiny as a pipe.

As an example of how the briar situation has changed over the years, in 1970 a sack of briar could realistically be expected to yield 5% of clean, top quality "firsts." Another 15% would become "firsts" that were suitable for sandblasting, a technique where tiny beads of glass, metal or sand are shot under tremendous pressure at a briar bowl, wearing away the softer wood and producing a hardened pipe with a durable ridged or mottled effect. Many high grades are sandblasted, a technique that requires a very fine grain in order to produce an attractive pattern. After selecting this 20% combination of smooth and sandblasted high-grade pipes, the bag might yield an additional number of pipes suitable for "deluxe seconds," a pipe that was on the borderline between a first and a second. In those days, the balance of the briar, for a high-grade company at least, would be considered worthless for pipemaking and the wood was simply discarded, a practice that is unthinkable today. But back then, it was a luxury in quality because briar was relatively inexpensive.

Today, however, due to the all-too-familiar specters of inflation, rising labor costs, plus the fact that few workers wish to "lower" themselves to the dirty sweaty job of digging for briar-root, prices have soared and pipemakers, in order to stay in business, find it an economical necessity to try and squeeze an extra 5% of "firsts" out of the same basic burlap sack they were using just ten years ago. Thus, the emergence of the "second-first" has become a reality.

Having a marketing and manufacturing creed of "Firsts Forever — No Seconds!" is both commendable and costly and can only be achieved in one of three ways: burn all the seconds, keep carving past the flaw until you either get a "first" or sand the pipe away to infinity, or develop a textured finish that relies on superb carving techniques rather than grain.

In light of the rising costs and scarcity of briar, it is reassuring to discover that many high-grade pipe firms not only continue to buy the very best plateau briar, but are also ready

Parts of the Pipe

CHAMBER   TENON   BIT   STEM   LIP   AIR HOLE   MORTISE   FERRULE   BOWL   SHANK

12

markets for Grade A and AA bowls that are occasionally obtained from other pipemakers. Additionally, it is an unacknowledged fact and up until now has been a carefully guarded secret, that many companies often produce bowls for each other. Personally, I cannot see how this matters one bit, as long as the end product is representative of the company's brand and the customer gets the quality he is paying for.

Once the *ebauchons* are selected and purchased by the buyers, they are delivered to their respective pipemaking facilities. Here they are usually sawn into L-shaped blocks, the first step of the long pipemaking process, a procedure that can involve from 80 to 120 different steps. The basics of carving a high quality pipe are shown photographically in this chapter. However, for those who would like to try making a pipe at home, there are a number of pipecarving kits on the market which can be acquired from your tobacconist. Just be sure to get a block with the air hole and tobacco chamber already drilled, for that is the most difficult part. However, if you really want to start from scratch and have lots of time on your hands, you could consider growing your own heath tree!

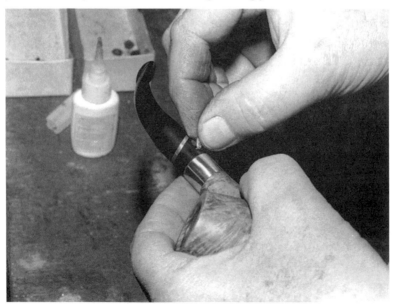

Pipe logos can be affixed by machine or by hand, such as this metal GBD logo being inserted into one of their high-grade pipes. By comparison, more popularly priced GBDs have their logos hot stamped onto the bit.

A pipe is fashioned into one of a number of basic and some not-so-basic shapes, much of which depends upon the design preferences of the individual pipemaker as well as the shape of the briar block. English and French companies normally tend to create "traditional" shapes while the Danish, Italian, and many of the German and U.S. custom carvers seem to lean towards "freehand" styles. The most popular of these designs are shown in the next chapter as an aid to pipe selection. However, no matter how it is shaped, there are three basic textures for any briar pipe: 1) smooth, 2) sandblast, and 3) carved or rusticated. A pipe may be finished in one or in any combination of these three textures.

A smooth finish is just what the name implies. It can be glossy smooth or matte finish and is usually found on pipes in which the grain of the wood plays an important part of the overall design. A smooth finished pipe can be oil cured and left in a natural shade or can be stained any color, from a light tan all the way to a deep brown and even black, depending on the wood and the whim of the pipemaker. There are even some pipes that are stained in non-traditional colors, such as green, but these are usually frowned upon by more experienced pipesmokers. Basically there are three types of grains

Silver mountings for pipes must first be formed on an exact wooden replica, such as this L&JS Ferndown silver cap being made for a billiard.

found on most smooth finished briar pipes: 1) straight grain, 2) flame grain, and 3) burl or bird's eye. It is not uncommon to find more than one type of grain on a pipe, such as when a bird's eye swirls around the bowl and turns into a horizontal straight grain on the other side. This type of double pattern is called a cross-cut; a horizontal grain is called a cross-grain. Some pipes have very little visible grain at all, while in others the pattern is more pronounced but is uneven, with no symmetry. This is referred to as a random grain. Many pipes even have "bald spots," in which the grain on the bowl is interrupted by a patch of smooth wood with little or no character.

The three basic pipe finishes (top to bottom): Smooth, shown on a Larsen pipe; sandblast, as seen on this Ashton Pebble Grain; and rusticated, on the Savinelli La Mia Pipa with a natural finish.

15

Normally, it is best to stay away from these pipes, for where there is no grain, there is little or no porosity. Then we have the flame grain, which is simply a straight grain pattern that angles either in or out along the bowl, giving it the very attractive appearance of a "flame." Finally there is a burl grain, which can be quite appealing if the pattern is pronounced and uniform. It is this individuality in graining that gives each piece of briar a personality all its own and makes one pipe more enticing to an individual than another.

Sandblasted pipes (sometimes referred to as shell, rustic, relief or thorn finishes by various manufacturers) are ruggedly attractive, with a roughened texture that makes you want to grasp the bowl firmly and rub your thumb over the wood, as there is no concern about marring the glossy waxed surface, as found on smooth-finished briars. Sandblasted pipes are somewhat lighter in weight because there is less wood on the pipe. Because there is actually more exposed wood surface area comprising the bowl, the heat from a sand-blast pipe is dissipated from the burning tobacco slightly quicker than with a smooth finished briar, but frankly, the difference is so slight as to be almost unnoticeable.

Many people are of the erroneous belief that a sandblast is an inferior pipe, but just the opposite is true. It actually

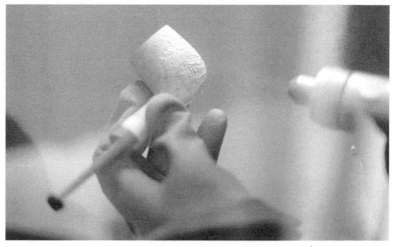

A popular alternative to the smooth finished pipe is sand-blasting, where a forced jet of tiny beads of sand, glass or metal is blasted onto the briar, etching away the soft portions of the wood and leaving a hardened, rugged surface.

takes a good grade of briar to create a truly fine sandblast, as the bowl must possess a better than average grain pattern in order to create the dimensional dips and ridges that make a sharply defined sandblast so desirable. One of the best examples of this is the deeply etched circular ridges of the Alfred Dunhill Shilling style of sandblast, which was introduced in the 1990s and like their earlier Ring Grain, is actually a perfect straight grain that has been sandblasted.

In addition to the wood, it takes a great amount of skill to properly sandblast a pipe. The coverage must be uniform and the ridges should not be too shallow or so deep they end up creating a misshapen pipe. I discovered all of these nuances firsthand when I was invited by William Ashton Taylor to sandblast a pipe at the Ashton factory in England. Holding a raw pipe bowl and thin nozzle that is angrily spewing out microscopic beads of sand at thousands of pounds of pressure per square inch is not an easy thing to do when your hands are covered with thick rubber gloves that are encased in a protective metal box. As a result, I ended up producing a rather strange looking billiard that had a very unique finger-resting ledge on one side of the bowl. Of course, I told Bill Taylor that this was exactly what I intended to do, when in reality I was thankful that I hadn't sandblasted right through my hand.

Unfortunately, sandblasting is also used by many pipemakers to cover up flaws and imperfections in a briar bowls that may be less than perfect. Because of this, sandblasts sometimes carry a stigma that is undeserved. For that reason, plus the fact that the grain is more easily seen and scrutinized on smooth bowls, sandblasts are less expensive than smooth pipes of the same quality.

Carved pipes include spot carving (normally employed to add a decorative touch to the bowl but more often than not, used to cut out or disguise a flaw in the wood), sculptured pipes in figural forms or designs, and freehands. Like smooth and sandblasted pipes, carved briars can be made either by hand or by machine but by their very nature, the more complicated designs are always made by hand. Do not confuse any variation of the high-grade carved pipe with the cheap imported varieties normally found next to the magazine rack in your local drugstore. Some examples of fully and partially carved quality pipes are shown elsewhere in this chapter.

Each carved pipe, no matter what its form, demands a certain skill, understanding of function, and expertise in its creation. For example, the freehand style, with its gently flowing curves and graceful, sweeping lines that ebb and surge throughout the pipe, show off briar grain to the fullest, but in so doing, exposes much more surface area of the briar and therefore runs the risk of uncovering many hidden flaws within the wood. The very intricacies of the designs themselves dictate that the freehand is usually a hand-carved, one-of-a-kind operation. On the other hand, a classical shape, such as a straight-stemmed billiard, must have visual and actual balance between bowl and stem to make it both functional and comfortable as a smoking instrument.

Detailed, carved pipes are often done by craftsmen using miniature electronic drills and dental tools which have been honed to a razor sharpness. "Rustication," a popular carving process that started in Italy and now has spread to England and other countries, is a technique whereby a pipe is skillfully poked and prodded with special multi-pointed tools that almost produce the appearance of a sandblast. When I first organized the National Pipe Carving Contest in America in 1976, I was amazed at the pipe craftsmanship that literally came out of the woodwork. After all these years I still find it fascinating to note the intricacies that a patient and skilled

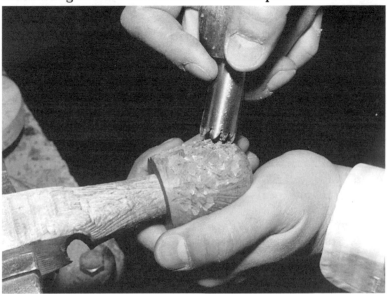

Another popular finish is rustication, which can be done with a special sharp tool or a chisel to create specific effects.

pipe carver can produce from a single block of briar, using just his hands and his imagination.

With the continuing quest for perfection in pipemaking, there has arisen a new breed of pipemaker, the true *artiste*. These individuals may only make from 25 to 500 pipes a year, but each one is an individually produced masterpiece. Most of these pipemakers make an annual pilgrimage to the Mediterranean briar fields, where they personally inspect and pick out each individual *ebauchon*, rather than purchase them by the burlap bagful, as is the standard custom. Of course, they pay infinitely more for each block of briar. But they literally have the very best briar obtainable. Their finished pipes reflect this exclusivity, and for some smokers, the cost is worth it. This custom pipemaking movement actually started in Germany, with pipemakers like Rainer Barbi, Karl-Heinz Joura, and Ingo Garbe; in Denmark with the grand master Sixten Ivarsson, Jess Chonowitsch, and Anne-Julie Rasmussen; and in North America with carvers such as Michael Butera, Julius Vesz, and Randy Wiley.

Whether carved by a single individual in his home workshop or in factories that turn out thousands of pipes each year for the pipesmoking world, each brand has its own feel and style, a certain "look" that gives the pipe individuality and character. Likewise, I have found that every pipemaker has a definite sense of pride in his craft, whether he is working alongside hundreds of others on a lathe in a factory or carving by himself alone in a room in his house. Practically all pipemakers of note strive to develop a certain "secret" or personal touch that will make their pipes stand out from the others. For example, Randy Wiley oil cures the insides of his bowls, an old-time technique that makes them extremely smokable from the very first bowlful; Clarence Mickles boils all of his cured *ebauchons* in water to further leech out any remaining impurities; and J.T. Cooke deep blasts his bowls to a point where you would swear they were hand carved.

But it is not just the smaller pipemakers who exhibit individuality. With its highly automated machinery, Stanwell produces very affordable high-quality pipes that were originally designed by such Danish artisans as Sixten Ivarsson and Jess Chonowitsch. Having been in continuous operation since 1858, the French firm of Butz-Choquin continues to create some of the most innovative designs of the 21st century. And from Ireland, Peterson has become legendary with its "Peterson System" reservoir under the pipe bowl and its unique Peterson Lip mouthpiece. Indeed, not only is briar the most smokable of all the pipemaking materials, but in terms of design and carving capabilities, it is also the most versatile.

Second in popularity as both a pipemaking and a pipesmoking material is meerschaum, which means "sea foam," and has the unique ability to change color as it is smoked over a long period of time, gradually turning from white to a deep cherry brown. The best pipes are made from solid block meerschaum, which is only found in Turkey. Interestingly, meerschaum of a slightly different texture is found in other parts of the world, including the United States and Africa, although most of it is not of pipemaking quality. However, the meerschaum product of the Dark Continent, while not as porous as the Turkish mineral, is effectively used for some oil-hardened or calcinated pre-colored pipes, most notably those that are fashioned on the Isle of Man, off the west coast of England, and sold under various pipe company names, such as Barling, Peterson, and Siyahi.

As a caveat to first-time meerschaum pipe purchasers, it should be pointed out that there are a number of imitation substances on the market, such as pipes made from powdered meerschaum scraps and synthetic polymers and resins. These pipes are always cheaper than block meerschaum and at first glance, may look like the real thing, but they offer none of the smoking qualities and coloring properties of the genuine article. "Pressed meerschaum" is sometimes used to line the bowls of inexpensive briar pipes, for which it is better suited.

Although not commonly known, Turkey's entire meerschaum supply is centered within a twelve mile radius of the tiny village of Eskisehir, located just 200 miles east of Istanbul. Here, in this single pinpointed area of the world, mine shafts poke as deep as 400 feet into the earth (often far below the water table of that area) and workers risk their lives in wet, subterranean shafts just to bring the pure, porous, and precious meerschaum chunks to the surface.

When the clumps of meerschaum are first brought up into the light of day, they must be cleaned of all dirt, sand, and other debris. The meerschaum is then sawn into blocks representing an approximate pipe-like shape. Many of these blocks are of a small to medium size, but occasionally an unusually large meerschaum chunk will be found, and these prizes demand extra attention, for with proper skill, they can

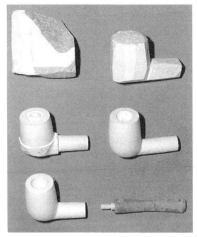

When making a meerschaum pipe, the grey-white block of meerschaum is first cut or turned into a rough shape of the pipe.

photos this page:
SMS Meerschaum

Next, the artisan carves his design in the soft, porous material. These carvings can be as intricate as the pipemaker's skill will allow.

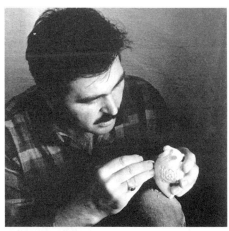

When the carving is finished, the meerschaum bowl is soaked in melted wax, which will aid in coloring the pipe as it is smoked.

21

be turned into a museum-quality showpiece. The basic pipe bowls are fashioned on a lathe, but one of the real attractions of meerschaum is its ability to be carved in great detail. This is made possible because of its relative softness. It is during this carving stage that an ordinary meerschaum pipe can be transformed into a true work of art. Yet, I have also seen some pipes whose intrinsic value had been totally destroyed by careless and unskilled butchering. Fortunately, few of these monstrosities ever find their way into a quality pipe shop.

Up until the 1960s, meerschaum pipes had been traditionally carved in Austria, with Vienna's Andreas Bauer being perhaps the best known in Europe and America. However, realizing a good thing when they saw it, in 1961 the Turkish government put an end to the exportation of raw meerschaum, thereby creating a captive pipe carving industry within her shores. Unfortunately, when Turkish-carved meerschaum pipes were first being exported in the 1960s and early '70s, the craftsmanship was not always the best quality. The mid-1980s and the '90s, however, saw a new breed of artisan emerge, exhibiting a much greater refinement and craftsmanship. That same skill is evident today. Thus, while we may probably never again see some of the classic European artistry on a commercial scale, over the past few years the skill of Turkish carvers has been steadily improving to a point of artistic excellence.

Besides being the world's sole source for Turkish block meerschaum, the area of Eskisehir is also home for the men who carve and shape practically every meerschaum pipe that will eventually find its way into your tobacconist's showcase. Specifically, most of the carvers live in a town that was formerly named Sebeci, but is now called Beyaz Altin, which means "white gold," because that is what meerschaum has become for this nation.

Some of the carvers in Beyaz Altin are true artisans with enviable skills, while others are simply people who happen to own a cutting tool and try to earn some extra money by attempting to whittle out a pipe or two in their spare time. In all of Turkey today, it is estimated that there are about 100 meerschaum pipe carvers of any note, of which only six are truly masterful experts, closely followed by less than two dozen talented apprentices. Perhaps the most recognized of these top carvers and the most heavily promoted in America is Ismet Bekler. Eyup Sabri is another of Turkey's true meerschaum sculptors; his intricate pipes feature carved mouthpieces made of water buffalo horn. Sabri has a unique system of triple-dipping his pipes in a specially-mixed wax solution that enables his meerschaums to color more rapidly than others, with noticeable changes occurring after only a few bowlfuls of tobacco.

It has only been recently that Sabri, a respected carver known as "The Artist" (whose real name is Ismail Ozel), and a few others have begun to actually sign their work. Most meerschaum pipecarvers rely on anonymous craftsmanship rather than the prestige of personal identity to sell their pipes, although that situation is changing, now that the names of the carvers are becoming known. But no matter who makes it, in a genuine block meerschaum pipe, price is determined not only by the size of the bowl, but also by the quality of the carving, and many an exquisite pipe has been fashioned by an unknown.

In spite of its rather fragile nature, meerschaum can be carved much like a briar pipe, although the delicate white "sea foam" must be kept moist, giving the material an almost cheese-like consistency, which therefore makes it much easier to work with and enables a skilled carver to create delicate facial features or intricate floral-leaf designs without chipping or otherwise destroying the material.

Once fully carved, the pipe is fitted with a stem and polished by hand with a finishing compound that smooths the surfaces. Then the bit is removed and the meerschaum is immersed in a boiling mixture of hot beeswax which is occasionally augmented with animal oils and fats. This beeswax bath gives the pipe a rich, yellow-tinged patina. However, as some pipesmokers seem to feel that a meerschaum pipe should be pure white, a fairly recent innovation has been to mix the beeswax with hydrogen peroxide, in order to bleach the meerschaum. Personally, I prefer the antiqued hue of just the beeswax, which actually helps color the pipe, as the bowl is already off-white. Although there is still a tendency to produce pure white meerschaum pipes with bleached beeswax, thankfully there is now a growing trend among many of the younger carvers towards the more natural look of pure wax.

Whether bleached or not, the pipe may undergo several dippings to insure that the entire area has been completely saturated with this boiling wax mixture, for it is the soaking of beeswax into the meerschaum surface that gives it the ability to change color. The better the saturation and more porous the meerschaum, the better the pipe will color when it is finally smoked; the nicotine and smoke from the burning tobacco seeps into the pipe, colors the wax and gradually works its way through the walls of the bowl to the outer surfaces. (That is why the thinner areas of a meerschaum pipe normally color first.) When dried, the newly waxed pipe is given a final polishing.

Most meerschaum bits are made of molded plastic of various hues, and attached with either a push-in or screw-on tenon. However, some carvers have recently reintroduced an amber bit on some of their better quality pipes and that glass-like material, once in vogue during the late 19th century, makes for a very handsome and aesthetically pleasing pipe, although it is more susceptible to breakage. Because of this, a few pipemakers are now using an amber resin, which is not so likely to crack.

Practically all meerschaums come in custom-fitted cases, which not only helps protect them during shipment, but is also invaluable in storing these fragile pipes at home. Back in the 19th and early 20th century, the cases used to be hand carved of wood and then covered with leather. Today they are form-molded of foam, and then covered with a synthetic material. Such is the mark of progress.

When completed, the pipes are put out for the representatives from one of the many meerschaum pipe companies who periodically visit the Eskisehir area on buying trips. The buyer carefully inspects each pipe and selects those which meet his criteria for style, craftsmanship and price. Occasionally, a meerschaum buyer will work with a select group of artisans whom he knows and can rely on, instructing them beforehand which designs he feels will sell well in his particular country. That explains how a craftsman in a remote Turkish village can suddenly be compelled to create a pipe dedicated to the personages of John Wayne or Sherlock Holmes, individuals he may never even have heard of. Finally, the pipes purchased by the various importing companies are sold via national salespeople to your tobacconist, who in turn offers you a selection of one of the earth's most unique natural smoking resources, the meerschaum pipe.

Of course, no discussion of the meerschaum would be complete without an addendum regarding the calabash. The calabash pipe is most often associated with the character of Sherlock Holmes, which is ironic since that legendary detective never once smoked a calabash in any of the sixty stories Sir Arthur Conan Doyle wrote about him. Nonetheless, the calabash is still one of my favorite companions when watching the old Basil Rathbone or Jeremy Brett reruns on television, or for any other form of "mysterious" at-home smoking.

The calabash originated in South Africa, and was introduced to England by soldiers returning home from the Boer War. In South Africa they had seen the locals smoking an unusual curved pipe made from a hollowed-out gourd. A little British ingenuity soon had the hot-smoking gourd fitted with a clay, and later, a meerschaum bowl. Some of the fancier versions were even mounted with silver or horn. And so the calabash was born as the 19th century was ending and the 20th century was beginning.

Basically, the calabash is a South African gourd which has been artificially shaped during the growing process to give it a gracefully hooked neck. After harvesting, the gourd is trimmed at both ends, hollowed out and dried. It is then polished, waxed, and fitted with a solid block meerschaum bowl, although some cheaper versions resort to crushed meerschaum or clay bowls; it is the solid block versions such as those made by Andreas Bauer and even an old Parker if you can find one, in which the gourd and the bowl will color as nicely as anything that ever was smoked in a Victorian sitting room or on the silver screen for that matter. The pipe is then fitted with a vulcanite or acrylic curved bit to complete its well-known profile. The calabash is a large and dramatically picturesque pipe and is not the sort of thing you want to cram into your coat pocket when going snowboarding. However, by the very nature of its construction, it is one of the few pipes in which all of the tobacco can be smoked right on down to the airhole in the bottom of the heel without any effort whatsoever. Furthermore, the air chamber of the inner gourd provides a cooling system that can help tame even the heaviest English blends. The calabash is truly a contemplative pipe and is best smoked at home on windy, rainy nights, when it can even turn a bad mystery book into a good one.

In dealing with the manufacture of all the popular pipes of the 19th century, how can anyone possibly ignore the humble corncob? It has been with us long before the Iron Horse first chugged across the buffalo-covered plains of the American West and it still remains a favored smoke in this era of DVDs and the internet. Surely the tenacious corncob must have something going for it.

If Saint-Claude, France is the pipemaking capital of the world, then the tiny town of Washington, Missouri must be the corncob capital of the world, for it is here that every corncob pipe is fashioned. But these historic little pipes are not created from your standard grocery store variety of corn, at least not anymore. In 1946, Dr. Marcus Zuber, working with the University of Missouri, developed a unique hybrid cob that was created specifically for use in pipemaking, and is now used exclusively by Missouri Meerschaum, the last remaining corncob pipe producer in the world.

The hybrid cob is larger, longer and stronger than your standard garden variety vegetable, and its fibers are so high in wood content that it takes a carbide-tipped saw to cut through them. The hybrid cob is grown by selected farmers in the rich, fertile lowlands that surround the town of Washington. The corn is grown strictly for the cobs they will produce and the small white kernels of the hybrids are regarded as a by-product (they are routinely sold off to companies who grind them up into cornmeal for tortillas; perhaps that explains why I always feel like smoking a pipe after a hearty Mexican dinner). It is the thick, sturdy corncobs which provide the real income for this area. Each fall they are harvested and trucked to the same old red brick building that has been the home of Missouri Meerschaum ever since 1872. Once inside, the cobs are "de-kerneled" and piled in a ventilated storage area, where they are aged for about two years, a curing process that gradually gives them the density of fine-grained hardwood. At the end of this period, the cobs are

These corncobs are made by Missouri Meerschaum, the last remaining manufacturer of this uniquely American pipe.

taken from the storage bins and sliced into various lengths for pipe bowls. An average cob will yield two standard sized pipes with a little left over for a miniature pipe with a one-inch bowl, the kind usually sold as novelties in souvenir shops. However, it is the more practical two-inch bowls that are favored by serious corncob smokers. Sometimes an unusually large cob will yield as many as five bowls, but these jumbo hybrids are often saved for long single-bowled pipes such as the General MacArthur style.

The cut cobs are then put on a lathe and shaped with a chisel, which gives the bowl its basic external design. The next step is boring the "tobacco hole," after which the cob is drilled for a stem and coated with a Plaster of Paris mixture very much unchanged from the original brew concocted for the first corncob back in 1868. This completes the bowl-making process for the least expensive pipes, such as the Standard model. Yes, there are high-grade corncobs! For this next step up, the bowls are hand varnished and shellacked and a tight-fitting wooden plug is hammered into the bottom of the bowl, which helps delay the burnout problem (you cannot build up a cake on a corncob). The stems used to be made out of riverbank reeds, but today the pipe stems are all fashioned from long rods of turned and drilled cobs. The one exception to this manufacturing procedure is the stem of the interestingly-christened Wanghee, which is actually the name of a variety of baby bamboo that is used to form the shank on this distinctive-looking Missouri Meerschaum. The pipe bits are molded of either clear or black plastic, depending upon the model of the corncob. There are more than fifteen different varieties of corncobs available, ranging from freehands to the most economically-priced seven-day set you will ever find in the new-pipe market. However, no matter what their size and shape, none of the corncobs are expensive. Their method of construction has remained basically unchanged for well over a century, thus giving this homegrown pipe a unique niche as a piece of American history that you can actually smoke.

Throughout the world of pipemaking, history is continually repeating itself as pipemakers insist on recreating pipes made of "alternate woods," such as manzanita, mountain laurel, ebony, rosewood, olive, cherry, birch, wild lilac and hickory, just to name a few. Everything has been tried, a fact that I often try to relate to many beginning pipemakers who come to me with their latest discoveries in smokable material.

Cherrywood pipes are rustic and smoke slightly sweeter than briar, but the wood is softer and more likely to burn.

Unless there is a unique substance growing in the canals of Mars, I am not aware of any other wood that can match the character and long lasting qualities of briar. However, it is only proper to give a nod of recognition to cherrywood as being the most popular non-briar wooden pipe today. Cherrywood provides a pleasant enough smoke, a little sweet in taste, but it burns hot at first, is more absorbent than briar, and being a softer wood, stands a greater chance of burning out. Consequently, it will not last as long. Cherrywood pipes are usually created in a rustic pot shape with the bark left on the bowl; a primary branch often becomes the stem. Thus, smoking a cherrywood is somewhat like smoking a miniature tree, a not altogether unpleasant experience.

Although most pipes are fashioned from natural materials, they almost always (with the exception of horn and amber) have bits that are of manmade substances. Most of these bits are made of either hard rubber (often referred to as vulcanite) or plastic (commonly called Lucite or acrylic, both of which sound a lot better from a marketing standpoint). Vulcanite was first used in 1878 and has become more or less a standard for many of the high grades. Because of the nature of the material, rubber can be carved into a wider variety of slimmer shapes, such as saddle bits, wide fishtail bits and even special bits for denture wearers. It is molded in cheaper pipes, but is actually handcut and shaped from long rods in the better brands. There are different qualities of rubber, with the best varieties today coming from Germany. Unfortunately, some of these supplies are now drying up, and many smaller pipemakers have already started stockpiling some of the great New York-Hamburg vulcanite. Because sulfur is a compound of rubber, vulcanite bits — no matter how good they are — will eventually oxidize and turn grayish white and even green if left in the sunlight or under fluorescent lights for any length of time. However, it is a simple matter to have the bit cleaned and buffed to a shiny like-new blackness, a task that many tobacconists and pipe repairmen perform for their customers regularly.

Compared to vulcanite, acrylic is a relatively new entrant in the pipe bit field. The Italian pipemakers of the 1960s and '70s should be credited for being largely responsible for popularizing the handcarved acrylic bit and bringing it into the world of elegant pipe fashion. Prior to the importation of their high design pipes, the plastic bit was primarily a simple molded affair. Now, some of the best

Making A Bit

With an acrylic pipe stem, first a sheet of the properly colored lucite is sawn to create a bar, as shown in this photo. In the case of rubber, a long round rod of vulcanite is sawn to length.

Next, the airhole is carefully drilled and the body of the bit and the tenon are turned to size on a lathe. Drilling the airhole is very exacting work, as the hole must be centered throughout the entire length of the bit.

Finally the bit is shaped by hand, using a series of files and polishing wheels.

shaped pipes sport handcut acrylic bits, often colored in elegant grays, blacks and amber hues, which will not oxidize. However, compared to rubber, acrylic bits are usually thicker and chunkier in design. This is due more to the manufacturing techniques of the pipemaker than to the material itself, for now, some pipemakers have started to trim their acrylic bits even thinner than before. Basically, acrylic is harder on the teeth than vulcanite, but a lot depends upon the personal preference of the smoker, the overall pipe design, and the balance of the bowl-to-bit ratio.

By its very nature, pipemaking is based on minutia, and some pipemakers, such as Germany's Rainer Barbi, America's Michael Butera, and Sweden's Bo Nordh, spend extraordinary efforts hand-sculpting the "button" (the tip of the mouthpiece) of some of their bits, which often have as many as five different angles to them. It is something that most pipesmokers do not even notice. A little more prominent is the strictly European design trend of blending briar, precious metals and even jewels into an acrylic stem, thereby creating a luxurious multi-tone effect. This technique can impart an elegant touch to a pipe, making it look equally at

Clay pipes are still made in the traditional way, using an antique mold with a thin wire inserted into the stem to form the airhole. The clay pipe is then air dried before it is fired in a kiln for final hardening.

home with a tuxedo, on board a yacht, or simply to lend a little class to a backyard barbecue.

There is one pipe that does not require any bit at all and that is the traditional clay. Lest you think that our old friends from the 16th and 17th centuries have shattered and disappeared from the pipe-smoking scene forever, they are still being made in England by Wilsons & Co. of Sharrow Ltd. (who took over the molds and operation from the old John Pollock Company) and a few tenacious individuals such as Stephen Bray of Olde World Fine Clays in Nova Scotia. These clays are still being made today in much the same manner and using many of the same molds (and in some cases, even the same type of clay) as when they were all the rage (in fact the only rage) in Europe and North America centuries ago. But as you might expect, the making of clays by traditional methods is not a mass production endeavor. At best, about six to seven clays can be made an hour, in order to risk not damaging and wearing out the already antiquated equipment.

The reason for the continuing popularity of the clay pipe is partly one of curiosity, mixed with a generous dose of

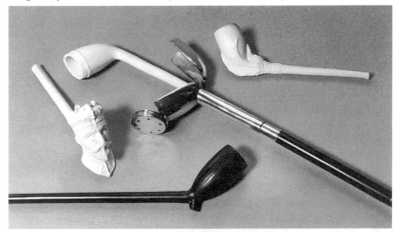

Clay pipes of the past are still available. Shown here is a figural bust of Britain's King George V and an Eagle claw shape #25, both imported by The Sheffield Exchange from Wilsons & Co. of Sheffield, England, which uses original 19th century molds. On the bottom is a graceful 16½-inch long 18th century Dutch Tavern Pipe made of ebony oil clay by Stephen Bray's Olde World Fine Clays of Nova Scotia, Canada. In the center is a rare original 18th century silver "pipe cane" with a ventilated cap.

nostalgia. After all, how else can one experience the same sensation that Raleigh or Dickens or Tennyson may have felt in another time, or know exactly what Watson meant when he spoke of Holmes' various well-smoked clays that littered that famous sitting room at 221B? And at our house at least, it is a Christmas tradition to smoke at least one bowlful of English blend in the old blackened churchwarden on the night of the 24th, before the last embers in the fireplace have died out. In addition, clays continue to be smoked by many historic re-enactors and are used by numerous universities for their various clubs and activities.

Just like briar, there were various grades of clay pipes. The Dutch pipemakers had three classifications: Regular, Fine and Porcelain, in which the pipe was finely burnished with an agate stone before firing and as a result, it had an extraordinarily smooth finish. In England, "Cream White," was known as the best and most desirable of clays.

To manufacture a clay pipe, the earthy substance is first soaked in water until it reaches a thick, dough-like stage; it is then rolled by hand into long thin strips. After the clay has started to "set," a thin wire is pushed through the length of the strip to form an airhole. The clay strip is then pressed into an oiled mold, which, when closed, compresses the clay into the shape of the pipe. An iron plug or sometimes even the maker's thumb is pressed into the bowl to form the tobacco chamber, which, of course, must connect to the airhole so that the pipe will draw. Some of the molds have engravings or decorations on them, which are embossed onto the pipes as part of their design. The entire wire, plug and clay ensemble are then clamped together and held under pressure. When the pipes have partly dried, they are released from the molds and a crafts-man takes a knife and carefully trims away any excess clay. At that time he also determines what the length and curva-ture — if any — the stem will have. Sometimes a maker's mark is carefully impressed into the bowl or the shank of the pipe to mark it. The clays are then fired in a brick kiln at a temperature of about 1050 degrees centigrade, after which a lacquer or colored varnish is painted on the tips of the pipe stems as in days of yore. Then the clays are care-fully packaged in either styrofoam or the more traditional straw and sawdust, and shipped out into the pipesmoking world of the 21st century, as an enjoyable reminder of our pipesmoking past.

In addition to the historic single-walled clay, a slightly more modern variation is the double-walled ceramic pipe — now rarely seen but still worth discussing, as they occasionally appear in various pipe shops. The double-walled ceramic clay was first invented around 1918 (and called "Old Mokum") by the Dutch van der Want family of the now-defunct Zenith pipe fame. This style of pipe features a twin-walled design with a hollow construction, somewhat on the calabash principle, except the entire bowl is of clay fired in a kiln, but only the outside is glazed; the inside of the bowl remains porous, so that it can absorb tar and smoke. As the pipe is puffed, the smoke circulates inside the airspace, which helps to cool it, and the double wall makes the pipe warm but not too hot to handle. The bit is a separate piece which is friction-fitted into the shank. One of the unique features about the double-walled pipe is that it can be decorated with beautiful floral designs, of which the Delft pipes are popular examples. The double-walled clay is also the only pipe which the manufacturers recommend cleaning with boiling water! Frankly, my prejudices built up over many years of pipesmoking make me shudder just thinking about this prospect.

Olivewood pipes from Italy offer a unique variation for today's pipesmoker. The blonde-colored wood turns matte-brown after the pipe has been smoked for a period of time.

But no matter what material a pipe is made of, whether briar, meerschaum or clay, it doesn't do the pipemaker any good unless he can sell it. Thus, one might wonder how these pipes get from the worker's bench and into the pipe shop. It is the end result of the manufacturing process and should therefore be reserved for the ending of this chapter. The pipes are sold through a series of large and small distributing firms, as well as by the individual pipemakers themselves. Traditionally, pipe salesmen make periodic calls on tobacconists around the country. However, each year the greatest concentration of pipe buying takes place at a number of tobacconist's "trade shows" held at various locations throughout the world. In the United States, the largest of these gatherings is at the Retail Tobacco Dealers of America trade show. Here, pipe shop owners gather to view the numerous tobacco products and pipes on display, to inspect and to buy for the upcoming season. Due to the popularity of pipe-smoking, it is a very competitive business, especially when a number of dealers are vying for the same limited supplies of perfect straight grains.

It is important to note that most of these pipe-selling conventions are for the tobacco trade only, as many products

One of the newest innovations in pipemaking is this Sardinian briar inlaid with cork by Italian pipemaker Tommaso Spanu. Perhaps this is one alternative to the sandblast, as the cork helps cool the smoke. The corkscrew belonged to cowboy actor Buck Jones.

are unveiled for the first time. The public must wait until the purchases are delivered to their local tobacconists to see what is available. However, the internet has now enabled many cyber-smokers to get a jump on the traditional pipe-buying season. Obviously, not all tobacco dealers will carry the same line of pipes or even charge the same price for the same pipe, so it pays to shop around for a particular brand or style you have in mind. Even so, I have found it to be personally much more rewarding to have one or two pipe shops that I patronize on a regular basis. After all, pipe buying is a highly individualized activity and once your tobacconist gets to know you, your smoking preferences and what you are looking for, he should be willing to keep an eye out for pipes that might fit your particular wants and budget when he is buying pipes for his store. And if you are looking for a specific pipe, it never hurts to ask your tobacconist if he can find it for you, either at the trade show, or by calling around to other stores. Most tobacconists, by the very fact that they are pipesmokers themselves, are friendly people and, if they are true professionals and believe in the spirit of the pipe (to say nothing of the spirit of customer service), they should be only too willing to help you find the pipe you want. But you have to know what you are looking for, and that is just what we will be discussing in the next chapter.

Chapter 2

PICKING A PIPE

One of the most pleasurable things you can do in the world today is to purchase a pipe. It doesn't have to be for any special occasion, but sometimes that helps. It could be your birthday, it could be someone else's birthday, or it could just be a good day for stepping into a pipe shop. Perhaps you want to celebrate something that happened, or console yourself over something that didn't happen. That's what pipes are for. They are friends, and like friends, you can never have enough of them.

The basic and unshakable rule for pipesmokers is to buy what you like and buy the best you can afford. That way, you'll never regret having made the purchase. But there is more to it than that. Today's pipe shops are well stocked with a multitude of brands and styles from all over the world. Unless you know exactly what you're looking for, it can be a bit confusing and even then, your tobacconist may not have the exact pipe you want, in which case you have to look elsewhere or settle

The image of the pipesmoker has always been admired by all creatures, great and small, as evidenced by this classic Ballard Street cartoon by Jerry Van Amerongen, one of America's most talented, perceptive, and enjoyable cartoonists. His works are syndicated in over 130 papers.
Copyright 1998
Creators Syndicate

for something else. But whatever the situation, there are decisions to be made.

If you are a new pipesmoker, you may want to start with a well made pipe in the medium price range, using it to learn the basic smoking techniques that we will be discussing in Chapter 3. Then you can upgrade with your next pipe purchase, although if selected wisely, a medium priced pipe will provide you with a lifetime of smoking pleasure. I still regularly smoke many of my earliest pipe purchases from college, as they were chosen with care, were well taken care of, and have mellowed with me through the years to the point where they now have the look and feel that is just not found on a new pipe. However, I have also outgrown some of these brands and styles, and thus, am continuously compelled to buy new ones.

If you are a seasoned pipesmoker, you already know what you like, but are probably always on the lookout for something new or different. A pipesmoker is never satisfied. I currently have more than 2,000 pipes in my collection (yes,

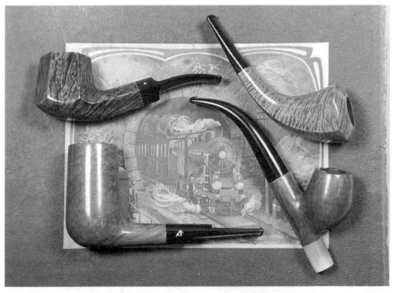

Like people, pipes come in a variety of shapes, and all of them are equally enjoyable. Clockwise from upper left: Comoy's Facet de Luxe six-sided panel; W.Ø. Larsen Pearl horn shape with paneled sides; Astleys cavalier from the original shop on Jermyn Street in London; an Ascorti King Size "stack."

I have let the hobby get slightly out of hand), but even today, acquiring a new pipe is still a magical moment for me. In fact, while photographing some of my newer personal pipes for this book, I couldn't wait to get the film developed so that I could finally smoke them (one must clean and polish the pipes beforehand and really shouldn't touch them until they have been photographed, so that they will look their best for the camera). Another interesting observation is that of all the pipes I own, there are about 50 that I keep in pipe racks and of those, there are only about 25 that I smoke on a regular basis. This, of course, points out the importance of picking your pipes carefully. After all, they are extensions of your personality.

By that same token, if you buy a pipe for a gift, you shouldn't buy what you like, but what you think the recipient might like. It also helps to take one's lifestyle into account. An outdoorsman might prefer a rugged pipe that he can put in his pocket. A fellow who must do a lot of business entertaining might be more prone to an elegant pipe with a silver or gold band. A person able to spend more time with his pipe would most likely appreciate a larger bowl for a longer smoke, whereas a university student might find a small bowl useful for half-hour sessions of relaxation

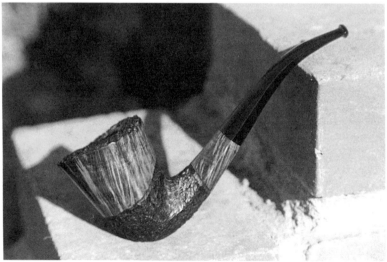

Some pipes have a combination of finishes, such as this Larsen semi-bent with both smooth and rusticated textures. Notice the evidence of natural plateau briar around the bowl rim.

between classes. Obviously, whether choosing a pipe for yourself or someone else, it is a very personal endeavor. However, there are some basic truths that will help make you a more informed pipe buyer.

First, most pipes come in one of two basic configurations, bents and straights, which is the terminology that refers to the shape of the shank and bit. A bent can have its "S" shaped configuration formed in any degree of curvature, from a very slight dip to highly exaggerated hook. The straight pipe can have a stem of any length, from very short and stubby to extremely long and slender. Normally, a bent pipe is easier for most people to hold in their mouths, as the center of gravity (i.e., the bowl) is lower and the pipe seems to "hang" better. Therefore, for individuals who like to talk with a pipe in their mouths, the bent is ideal. The straight is more traditional and urbane and is quite practical for me, as I often use my pipe as a pointer when conducting pipe and whiskey seminars or when speaking at pipe dinners. Also, the straight pipe tends to keep the bowl (and hence, the smoke) a little farther away from my face. However, I have been clenching straights and bents in my teeth for years with equal aplomb and the only comment I ever received regarding this practice was from my dentist, who mentioned that I have

Elegance in briar — Davidoff pipes come in three finishes: black sandblast; red double stained; and bright natural. The sterling silver pipe rest is by D.W.D. of England.

extremely well developed jaw muscles (great for cracking walnuts with your teeth). Most pipesmokers have both styles of pipes in their collections. Interestingly, in the past the ratio was bents over straights by a 3 to 1 margin, but nowadays, more pipesmokers are gravitating towards straights so the current margin is closer to 50-50 between the two.

Both bent and straight pipes come in a variety of shapes, ranging from classical and conservative to modern and *avant-garde*. And no matter what the shape, the pipe size can be extra small (more common in Europe than America) to extra large. However, most pipesmokers seem to settle on the practical medium sizes, which tend to hold enough tobacco for a 45-minute smoke. To help make pipe selection easier, some companies, such as Peterson, Davidoff, and Brebbia, issue catalogs with "shape charts," which unfortunately are not as common as they once were. It is just as well, for many of the

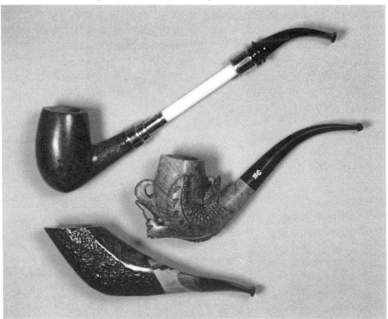

Three centuries of Butz-Choquin pipes (top to bottom): the Origine, one of the very earliest designs made by B-C. The pipe originally used an albatross bone for the stem, although today it is made of plastic; carved eagle claw, shape #105, which is very similar to the early Saint-Claude carvings of the 19th century; and the ultra-modern Cybèle, with its multiple layers of contrasting woods and textures.

41

old standard pipe shapes have been given new names, and this can sometimes be confusing to the neophyte pipeologist trying to get a handle on things. Although I have personally categorized over forty different pipe shapes (with many of the same shapes having more than one name, depending on how many pipe companies are making it), I have attempted to simplify things a bit by reducing this entire battalion of appellations down to eight basic styles, which you can use to help get your message across to any tobacconist when he or she asks, "What type of pipe are you looking for?" They are:

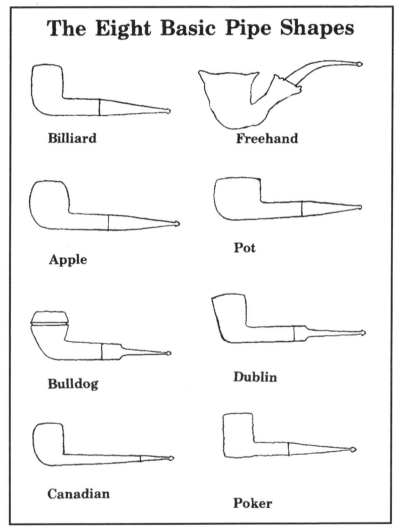

The Eight Basic Pipe Shapes

Billiard

Freehand

Apple

Pot

Bulldog

Dublin

Canadian

Poker

1. **BILLIARD**: The classic traditional straight pipe, often with a fairly good-sized bowl in relationship to its size. The definition of a proper billiard is: "The height of the bowl equals the length of the shank."

2. **APPLE**: A graceful pipe with a round bowl that appears to have been flattened slightly. The stems of apples can be either straight or slightly bent. The Apple shape first appeared in the 1920s.

3. **BULLDOG**: A bowl characterized by a carved band around a swelling circumference, about a third of the way down from the rim. Bulldogs usually have a diamond-shaped stem, giving them a sporty appearance. Bulldog bowls can be either squatty, medium, or tall. They are a very handsome, outdoors-looking pipe and one of the most difficult shapes to make.

4. **CANADIAN**: A straight pipe with a longer-than-usual shank and a comparatively short bit. There are fewer Canadians made than other styles, as the design requires a piece of briar that will fit the requirements of the long shank. Consequently, these pipes are often in demand by collectors. Years ago, the Canadian shape was also called a Lumberman, but you rarely hear that term today.

5. **FREEHAND**: Any pipe in which the shape seems to be sculpted, rather than following traditional designs. Companies like Charatan were making freehands well before WW II, but it was the Danish who made freehands popular, beginning in the 1960s. These pipes are often referred to as freeforms in Europe.

6. **POT**: A pipe with a wide, short, flat-topped bowl and a rounded bottom. Pots were first made in the 1930s. People either love them or hate them. There is rarely a middle ground with this shape.

7. **DUBLIN**: An old design in which the bowl gently angles up from the stem so that the top is noticeably wider than the bottom.

8. **POKER**: A cylindrical self-standing pipe which has its stem slightly above ground level of the flat-bottomed bowl.

These are the most readily-encountered shapes you will find in most pipe shops. Obviously, there are many more styles, like the curved Oom-Paul, a deep bent with a tall bowl and which was named after Paul Kruger, South Africa's patriot of the Boer War; the Lovat, basically a shortened Canadian that was inspired by a Scotsman named Lord Lovat; and the ever-popular Prince, a graceful, slightly bent pipe with a small, rounded bowl designed for the Prince of Wales in the 1920s. Ironically, it was rumored that he never seemed to care for this shape. In addition, there is the slabsided Panel, the Rhodesian (which is really a round-shanked bent bulldog) and a host of variations upon existing shapes, such as oval bowls and pipes with square shanks so that they can stand up without falling over.

Throughout this book you will find photos of most of the shapes available to the known world. If you see a particular pipe shape that you like, take this book to your tobacconist and show him the picture. Lots of my readers do it. I will never forget the time I was in the tiny bar of The Lochalsh Hotel on the west coast of Scotland, having a few pints with the locals on my way to visit some of the malt whisky distilleries. As a

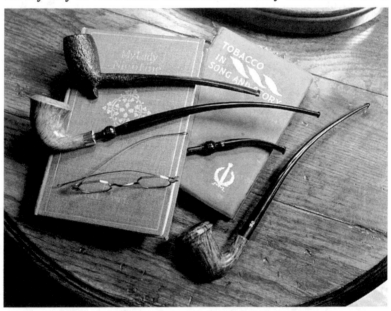

Some pipes are designed for smoking at home, such as these long-stemmed churchwardens (top to bottom): Dunhill Group 4 Cumberland made from an old bowl found in the warehouse; Stanwell Hans Christian Andersen, which comes with an extra, smaller bit; and a Butz-Choquin Calabash Jr.

number of us were smoking our pipes, the conversation gradually drifted to that topic.

"I'll bet you can't tell me what kind of pipe that gent in the corner is smoking," one of the locals challenged me. He pointed to a stranger at the far end of the room. The man was smoking one of the very pipes that was depicted in my British pipe book and, of course, I recognized it instantly.

"I'll bet you a pint that not only can I tell you what kind of pipe it is, I will also tell you the name of the man who made it," I said, as I boldly walked over to the individual, who looked up in surprise.

"You, Sir," I said, "are smoking a briar-ribbed 'Skipper,' which was made in Denmark by a man named Eric Nørding."

The pipesmoker dropped his jaw and almost dropped his pipe.

"Blimey," he said, "you're right!" And then he recognized me. "I've got your book!" he said, jumping up out of his chair. "I saw this pipe pictured in it, took it to my tobacconist, and told him to get me a pipe just like it. And he did!"

And thus, I won a pint of bitters. So you can see the power of the pipe.

Because the most popular pipes are made of briar, which is the king of smoking materials, let's discuss these pipes first in discovering how to select the best smoking instrument for our money. From Chapter 1 we already know that briar pipes come in three different finishes: smooth, sandblast and carved. Smooth finished pipes are by far the most popular and it is through our understanding of how a pipe is made that we can now select a quality briar.

Generally, smoking ability depends upon how well the briar has been cured (dried), and how well the pipe has been made. The things to examine are 1) is the tobacco hole centered in the bowl, 2) does the airhole from the stem enter the bowl at the bottom of the tobacco chamber so that all of the tobacco can be smoked, and 3) how has the pipe been finished? If the tobacco chamber is off-center, then one side of the bowl will become hotter than the other and you have a good chance to scorch or burn through the wall of the pipe. If the airhole is too high, it indicates sloppy workmanship, and where there is one thing wrong, there is likely to be another.

But what about the curing of the wood? Generally, the lighter a pipe weighs, the more thoroughly it has been cured and freed of resin and moisture, although be sure to take bowl size into consideration. A properly cured large freehand will

When considering the purchase of a pipe, carefully examine the inside walls of the bowl. This model from an otherwise reputable manufacturer has an unforgivable flaw which would invariably have caused a burnout. Don't buy it!

Always check the bowl to make sure the airhole comes out at the exact bottom of the heel. This airhole has been drilled off-center, indicating sloppy workmanship that will translate into an unpleasant smoke and an uneven cake.

By contrast, this pipe by American carver Mike Butera exhibits exemplary workmanship, with a smooth, evenly turned tobacco chamber and a properly positioned airhole.

naturally weigh more than a small apple design. When choosing a smooth finished briar pipe, the grain and quality of the wood is the all-important criteria. As a rule, the older the briar, the closer and more pronounced the grain pattern will become. In a sandblast, the older the briar the rougher the surface. This roughness can be shallow or deep, depending on how the pipe was sandblasted. A lightly sandblasted pipe is not necessarily an inferior pipe, although most smokers, especially in America, prefer deep etching.

All well-made briar pipes have a natural oil or stained finish. The bowl should never be painted or lacquered, processes that can hide flaws in the wood and which seal it, thereby preventing the pipe from breathing, a necessary ingredient in obtaining a cool smoke. Very inexpensive drugstore pipes should be avoided. We've all seen them, piled up in a box on the tobacconist's counter and usually selling for less than the price of a box of matches. While these barrel-pipes, as they are sometimes called (because years ago they were sold from a barrel), may be "smokable" in a literal sense of the word, few of them can give the pleasure that a pipe

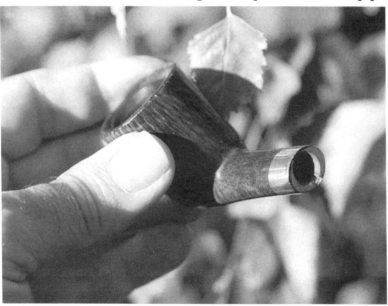

For collectors of estate or "pre-smoked" pipes, it is important to note that a non-factory band may sometimes have been put on to repair a cracked shank. It is always best to take off the bit and check.

person deserves. Those cheap imitations of the real thing normally have a varnished or lacquered, puttied-up finish and as a result, they produce an extremely "hot," tongue-biting smoke that is often accompanied by a gunky, wet acidic taste, caused by the heat being trapped inside the sealed walls of the bowl. These poorly-made pipes have turned more people away from pipesmoking than a room full of anti-smoking zealots. Thus, many a would-be pipesmoker has given up the practice without ever realizing the full pleasure that could have been obtained from a properly-finished briar. Therefore, be sure you buy only naturally stained briar.

Even though we are looking for quality, you don't necessarily have to spend a lot of money for a good pipe, although like most things in this world, you usually get what you pay for. However, pipes by Stanwell and Peterson have made their very substantial reputations by providing excellent smoking values for the money, and some of them, like the Stanwell Year

The criteria for a woman pipesmoker is the same as for a man. The pipe must be of a practical size, it must look good, and it must make *her* look good!

Pipes and various Peterson commemoratives, actually have become quite collectable. As another example, although both

One of Stanwell's newest shapes, #217, exhibits perfect harmony of Danish elegance and styling in a straight grain.

Peterson's old and new (clockwise from upper left): currently-made Peterson 1905 Antique reproduction with case; Peterson original bulldog from 1905; Peterson "Hand-Made" re-issue of their house pipe; and Peterson shape 356 from the early 20th century, a style that is still being made today.

Nørding and Larsen are known for their high quality briars, both Danish firms also produce excellent pipes in the lower price ranges.

There are also bargains to be found if you get lucky or know what to look for. Very often a tobacconist will have special sales on certain high-grade pipes, off-brands or close-outs. Some top-of-the-line brands, however, are rarely discounted. On the other hand, if you are a pipe connoisseur or collector/smoker who gravitates towards perfect straight grains or Danish freeforms, there is practically no limit to the amount you can spend and the quality you can buy, especially if you enjoy smoking the limited edition masterpieces carved by some of the American, German, and Danish new wave artisan-pipemakers. But no matter what the pricetag on a pipe, the quality of the briar and the skill of the workmanship has a direct effect upon its cost. Therefore, we must know how to pick the best pipe within its price range.

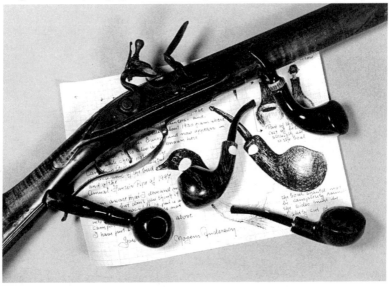

Erik Nørding's Hunting Pipes of the Year pay seasonal tribute to popular wild animals and gamebirds. Each limited edition pipe comes with a detailed drawing and description by artist Mogens Andersen. (L. to R.) 1999 quail; 1997 Canadian goose (shown with accompanying description sheet); 1995 pheasant (this was the first year of issue); and the 1996 Sitka deer. The author's 1790-styled flintlock hunting rifle was made by Judd Brennan.

Unfortunately, not all pipes are made of well-cured briar. I would like to tell you differently, but I have encountered a few "new" pipes made of wood that smelled green. By that, I mean the inside of the bowl had a wet, musty odor. And upon smoking the pipe, it was harsh, hot, and wet, which means that the briar had not properly cured. Thankfully, this is not usually encountered, but when it is, I waste no time in telling both the tobacconist and the pipemaker of this problem. On the other hand, good, well-cured briar is the only type used by all of the better pipemaking firms, most of whom place a premium on grain design.

When studying the grain on a pipe, the main thing to look for is symmetry of pattern. While a perfect straight grain is always more desirable from an aesthetic point of view, it does not affect the smoking quality of a pipe. The main criteria for a good smoking pipe, as far as grain is concerned, is total bowl coverage, no matter what the grain pattern. Stay away from pipes with bald spots that could lead to a hot spot and consequently in time, a burn-out, which will actually produce a hole in the wall of the bowl.

As we stated in the last chapter, a "first" is the *ne plus ultra* of owning a briar pipe, but you must expect to pay for the privilege. In today's pipemaking world of rising labor

This sophisticated briar was made by Cesare Barontini for Calabresi and features a square silver mounted shank. All it needs is a pipesmoker in a tuxedo.

costs and a growing unavailability of suitable briar, many pipes are being sold as "firsts" with minor pitting or surface blemishes. Only you can decide if the pipe is worth the price. If your budget and your personality both suggest that you smoke only "firsts," by all means do so, as they are good investments as well as being superb sources of pride.

Of course, there is absolutely nothing wrong with "seconds." They occupy the majority of spaces in most pipe racks including my own, and I guarantee I will be acquiring

Danish pipemaker George Jensen offers a wide variety of affordable shapes. (top to bottom): straight-stemmed Oliver with olive wood trim; Macon #51 matte finish with gold band; and "Kontrast" shape #95 sandblast with a smooth top and briar inset dot in the mouthpiece. The pipe tool was made from a 19th century pearl handled fruit knife by D.W.D. of England.

many more "seconds" before the last match flickers over my final bowlful of Latakia. "Seconds" are notably less expensive than "firsts" and are usually made from the very same wood. The only difference is that a few imperfections are present which may or may not be apparent to the casual observer and which in no way affects the quality of the smoke. Moreover, by going to a reputable tobacconist and knowing your pipe brands, it is possible to purchase seconds that are made by some of the world's premium pipemakers. The Parker brand was originally started in 1923 by Alfred Dunhill as a means to sell their "seconds," and Tilshead are James Upshall "seconds," just to give two examples.

In addition, many of the top pipemaking companies have seconds that are marketed under a variety of "private label" names. This is nothing more than an exclusive name for a pipe (in fact, they are often called "exclusives") that is reserved for a specific tobacco shop or a chain of stores. Most pipe factories will even make up a die and stamp a tobacconist's "exclusive" private label on the stem if a sufficient quantity is purchased by the shop. Other tobacconists have stamping machines that enable them to emboss their own private label names directly on the pipes in their store. It is a great adventure to discover some of the many off-brands that proliferate the market, as these briars can represent some of the best values in the pipesmoking world if your tobacconist has lucked into an unusual find. The unknown pipe of today may be the hot new brand of tomorrow. The

After an absence of many years, Italy's Lorenzo pipes are back, with a variety of handmade and machine-made stylings.

Italian brand of Don Carlos started this way. When they were first imported into America a few years ago, no one had ever heard of them. But soon the word got out that the wood was exceptionally good for the prices charged. Now, of course, they are hard to keep in stock and unfortunately, the prices have risen somewhat, but they still remain good smoking pipes. Balleby is another example; when I first wrote about this brand in *Rare Smoke*, no one had ever heard of it. Now they are being imported into the U.S. and while not inexpensive, have become one of the trendy new pipes.

Recently there has been a great deal of renewed interest in some of the more established Italian pipes, such as Mastro de Paja, Ser Jacopo, Radice and Ascorti, as well as some of the newer Danish and German brands, resulting in an increased demand for their products. However, in the case of the Danish and Italian pipes, it is important to realize that their concept of a "first" differs from the U.S. and British definition: a Danish or Italian "first" may have minor sand pits — "nature's way," they say. It is the quality of the briar and the grain that they look at. That is why a top-of-the-line Castello Collection Greatline Fiamata can cost thousands of dollars, even though it may have a few pinpoint sand spots on an otherwise superbly-grained finish. This is contrary to the school of thought that states a smooth "first" must, by definition, be completely free of blemishes, as evidenced by a Butera Royal Classic or an Alfred Dunhill root briar. In addition to the purity of the briar, many high-grade pipes also sport gold or silver bands, which adds to both the beauty and their value.

Although I personally like to see the quality of the wood graining inside the bowl as well as outside, some pipemakers pre-carbonize their bowls as an aid to breaking them in. Depending upon the substance used, this can actually have a positive effect, or it can be strictly cosmetic. The reality is that no amount of artificial carbonization can equal the thickness nor effectiveness of a natural cake that has been built up over four or five bowlfuls. More about this in the next chapter. And borrowing upon the technique of some pipemakers who used to line their briar bowls with clay in the 19th and early 20th centuries, a few pipes are made today with meerschaum-lined bowls. The thought here is that because meerschaum pipes need no breaking in, you bypass this step when lining the briar bowls with this substance. It is, at best, a compromise and for pipesmoking, the purest of the smoking arts, compromises never give complete satisfaction. For one thing, the meerschaum used is not high-grade "block," but

An elegant non-filter handmade Reiner Design pipe from Germany, shown leaning against the author's knighthood sword. This was the pipe he smoked during his knighthood ceremony in Miltenberg.

Two variations from db Design Berlin: (top) handmade Premier, shape 46S with silver mountings, and (bottom) a Danish-styled Geneva with lucite accent in the mouthpiece. Unlike the majority of db pipes, the relatively narrow shanks on these models verify that neither pipe has a 9mm filter and hence, were made for the American market.

is made up of pulverized and sometimes synthetically altered meerschaum, so the smoke does not have the porousness and coolness that one would find in a "real" meerschaum pipe. For another, the briar of these pipes is often not of the best quality and therefore does not "breathe" as a normal briar pipe would. Finally, because there is a meerschaum liner between the tobacco and the briar bowl, you are not able to taste the wood (yes, briar does have a taste, depending on the type used) and the pipe is not permitted to color and achieve that all-important seasoning that can only come after smoking numerous bowlfuls of tobacco in an all-briar pipe.

Even so, the only briar pipes I would suggest avoiding altogether are "thirds" — pipes made of poor quality briar and exhibiting noticeable putty "fills" — patches in the wood that literally have been filled and disguised with coloring to try and match the wood. Putty suggests a serious flaw in the briar, which means you are asking for potential disappointment after you have smoked a few bowlfuls. Normally, a "fill" is an indication of a weak spot in the briar and if located on the bowl, could indicate a possible danger of burnout, a situation where a hot spot of tobacco actually burns through to the

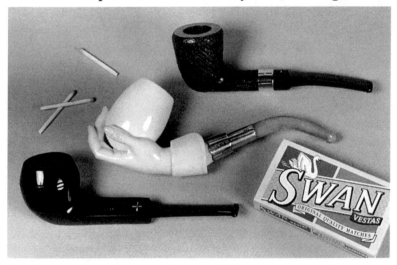

Barlings old and new: (top) gold-banded smooth-topped shape #4729; (bottom) Guinea Grain bulldog; (middle) a rare Victorian silver mounted original Barling meerschaum with amber stem. The new Barlings are available with a convertible tenon for smoking with or without a 9mm crystal filter.

outer bowl. From an aesthetic standpoint, fills are unsightly and even if stained to match the rest of the bowl, putty will not color like briar as it is smoked and therefore, will become even more noticeable as time goes on. Because a "third" is an imperfect pipe, it stands to reason that the manufacturer did not take as much time and care in making it. Thus, we go back to our basic rule for pipe buying: obtain the best you can comfortably afford.

On more than one occasion I have heard various people advising a first-time smoker to buy a meerschaum pipe, as "sea foam" requires no break-in. I do not feel that this is practical advice. While meerschaum is noted for providing a smooth smoke right from the start, the naturally fragile nature of the material requires that it be handled with extra care, which includes not touching the bowl as it is being smoked. This, to my way of thinking, takes away a lot of the spontaneity associated with pipesmoking, especially for the newcomer in our ranks. Therefore, I heartily recommend a briar pipe for a first purchase, saving meerschaum as a well-deserved "alternative smoke."

Like any other pipe, when buying a meerschaum the basic rule applies: seek out quality. There are actually different grades of meerschaum, but by the time they are made into pipes, it is difficult to tell them apart. But one must assume that a carver who has pride in his work would not waste his skill on an inferior block of meerschaum. In addition, because meerschaum has no grain, you must console yourself by looking for shape and being very critical as to the quality of the carving, even if it is a smooth pipe. Because most meerschaums are produced by the same basic coterie of Turkish carvers, you may find similar pipes sold under a variety of importers' names. Meerschaums are priced according to the size of the bowl and the degree and quality of carving the pipe exhibits. Even a smooth and polished meerschaum without any carving at all is a very attractive pipe and will color just as well as a carved version, although without all of the intricacies of the darker brown cracks and crevices where the tobacco juices and smoke have permeated first. However, there are some meerschaums that will simply not color. I have a favorite meerschaum, a large ornately carved bent, that I have smoked for years, but it has never progressed beyond a pale tan. Of course, the inside of the bowl has colored beautifully! Still, I keep on trying, varying my tobaccos and hoping to get lucky, because coloring ability aside, it is a superbly smoking pipe.

It is strictly a matter of personal taste as to what style of meerschaum pipe you choose. Just be sure you obtain a pipe that is carved of solid block and not the cheaper grade of meerschaum dust which will not smoke as cool or color as well. The buyer of such imitations loses on two of a meerschaum pipe's most important attributes: appearance and smokability.

Although the standard carved block meerschaum pipe has been with us since the 18th century, around 1980 a new type of meerschaum made its appearance and has caught on with a number of smokers. However, its availability is often quite limited. It is called the Manx meerschaum, a pipe made from the African product rather than the Turkish. Thus, it is slightly harder and not as porous. These pipes have been further hardened (or "calcinated") by heating them in oil and some are artificially colored to look as if they have been smoked for years. They are sold under various brand names,

The many faces of meerschaum: In the foreground, a currently made Turkish meerschaum just starting to color. Behind it is an unsmoked Austrian traveling pipe with amber stem and 14kt. gold mounts. To the right is a superbly carved Bacchus from the 19th century. Behind the pipe is an embroidered Victorian smoking cap.

including Barling, Peterson, and Siyahi. Calcinated pipes are heavier than standard meerschaums, but still lighter than briar. They are quite attractive and cool smoking and unlike block meerschaum, they can be handled while they are hot without mottling the color and they are not nearly as fragile.

Clays, on the other hand, are the most breakable of all pipes, and it is easy to see why they were so enthusiastically replaced by briar in the mid-19th century. Still, smoking a clay pipe is the closest thing to time travel we are likely to experience. They are an enjoyable smoke for the historically-inclined and I use clay pipes for much of my tobacco testing, as they give the purest of smokes. Also, like briar, in time a good clay pipe will season, and gradually acquire a wonderful off-white patina. However, they do smoke hot and have to be held by the stem, in true European fashion. There are only a few clay pipe makers left in the world and due to limited demand, many tobacconists no longer stock them. But they are available. Wilsons of Sharrow in England still uses original Victorian molds, while Stephen Bray of Olde World Fine Clays in Nova Scotia uses historically correct duplicated molds from the 1700s and actually has composed an exact

Manx meerschaums, such as this Barling made on the Isle of Man, are oil hardened and colored to give even the newest pipe a well-smoked look.

recreation of the clay that was used three hundred years ago. He even recreates the famous black clays of old by putting wood chips into his firing kiln. In addition, while touring Colonial Williamsburg, I was delighted to find that clays are still being made, sold and smoked in that historic part of the country. Most of the existing manufacturers offer everything from short-stemmed cutties all the way up to long, elegant churchwardens.

In buying a clay, the first thing to do is to make sure it wasn't broken or cracked in shipping. Then check to see that the airhole is clear. And rather than buy one clay, I would purchase two, just in case the cat decides to play with the first one during the night.

Because corncobs are so distinctly American, we should give them a patriotic nod of recognition. It is effortless to buy one. Basically, a corncob is a corncob. There is no grain to worry about, no aging factor to consider, and very often the pipe will cost less than the tobacco you put in it. Our only concern is to find a shape that you like. Corncobs are more or less standard in design, but there is the dramatically large MacArthur and even a freehand model. Corncobs are highly absorbent and should have their shanks cleaned regularly, smoked slowly, and allowed to completely dry out for a few days between smoking sessions. Treated this way, a corncob can last for years. In fact, the biggest concern with a corncob is if you leave it somewhere, should you take the time to go back for it or simply buy a new one?

In perusing the tobacco shops, you may occasionally come across a few unconventionally-designed briars that are called "trick pipes" in the trade. They always have an unusual gimmick or two about their construction. Some examples are vest pipes with fold-away stems, pipes with built-in spring-loaded tampers affixed to their bowls, pipes that smoke upside down and other such abnormalities. Most of these are smokable to various degrees, and it is up to the individual to decide whether or not such a pipe is for him. I personally prefer the more traditional versions.

When considering which pipe to buy, we must not become so concerned over the style, size and grain structure that we forget the part that we will come into closest contact with: the bit. If the pipe doesn't fit our mouth correctly, we are not going to enjoy smoking it. More than one repairman has made a good business out of reshaping pipe bits for customers.

As we know from reading Chapter 1 (or did you skip directly to this chapter first? Shame on you.), most bits today are made of hard rubber (often referred to as vulcanite, an older term stemming from the last century) and plastic or hardened acrylic, which ranges from the inexpensive molded bits found on the cheapest pipes all the way up to the hand-cut glossy Lucite used for the very best of briars. Vulcanite is softer on the teeth than acrylic and is a more traditional material. However, if not buffed after each smoking and allowed to be exposed to sunlit for any length of time, rubber will oxidize and turn grayish white in time. Fortunately, these bits can be professionally cleaned and polished to a like-new luster by your tobacconist.

On the other hand, Lucite will never tarnish and does not lose its color around the oxidized "bite marks" on the bit. Because it is harder than rubber, Lucite will take longer to bite through if you use a hard "chomp" to hold your pipe in your mouth. It will break, however, just as rubber will, especially at the tenon, one of the most fragile parts of a pipe. Additionally, many pipemakers continue to fashion even their most expensive pipes with thicker Lucite bits, when with a

Georges Simenon 1903 - 1989

Pipesmokers in fact and fiction — A Swiss-made Bentley "Former's Design" saddle bit bent is shown with Georges Simenon commemorative postmarks, which indirectly pays tribute to Simenon's creation, the pipesmoking Inspector Maigret. The pen is a Mont Blanc Alexandre Dumas limited edition that honors another great writer.

61

little care, they could be making these mouth pieces much thinner and more comfortable. However, Lucite offers interesting pipe design possibilities, as evidenced by some of the inlaid designs found on some Italian pipes, or the multicolored swirls occasionally used by pipemakers such as Larsen.

In addition to rubber and acrylic, occasionally you may encounter some of the more expensive pipes with bits made of horn or amber. Horn bits were once quite popular in the 19th and early 20th centuries. However, they are relatively soft and can chip, although they do lend a nostalgic elegance to any pipe. Amber is undergoing a renaissance and is occasionally being found on some of the better quality meerschaums and more unusual high-grade briars. Amber is actually fossilized prehistoric plant resin which is found along the southern shores of the Baltic Sea. It comes in colors that range from off-white to yellow to a rich, deep red. Interestingly, when it was first used, it was the clear amber that was the most expensive and desirable. However, in the 1960s when many pipemakers started using clear plastic in their bits, it made the clear amber look cheap. Consequently, today it is the gold and reddish shades that are most sought after. Amber is opaque and glass-like in structure and consequently, can break quite easily,

Many pipesmokers confuse real amber with the colored translucent acrylic that is more commonly found on meerschaums. Real amber will usually have a sticker somewhere on the pipe telling you that it is the genuine article. But there is also a powdered version of this material that is molded in a resin base. It is somewhat harder than pure amber, but lacks the clarity. A better compromise is Ambrolith, a higher grade of synthetic amber being made in Germany from a resin that is being used by a few custom pipemakers whose clients can afford this costly material. Of course, there are still some custom pipemakers, such as Canada's Julius Vesz, who have a very limited stock of real amber, and pipes with these bits are priced accordingly. Both horn and amber have an old world mystique that predates Lucite or vulcanite, although I feel these latter two materials are far more practical for pipe stems.

Most stems are affixed to their shanks by one of three methods:

Push Stem — this is the most commonly found. It is put on and removed with a gentle twisting motion. This should only be done when the pipe is cool; otherwise the shank could crack. Just as a matter of habit and my own sense of orderliness, I prefer to twist the stem on in a clockwise manner and off with a counter clockwise motion, but it really doesn't matter, unless the push-tenon is a separate piece screwed into the bit. If so, then the bit should always be removed with a clockwise motion, to avoid loosening the threads of the tenon.

Threaded — normally found on the acrylic stems of meerschaums. The threaded tenons are usually made of plastic, although some, especially on older pipes, are fashioned of bone. Just be sure, when properly tightened, the bit lines up perfectly with the shank and the "button" is horizontal to the bowl.

Military Mount — These are commonly found on pipes such as the Peterson but there are others as well. The military bit is friction-fitted, with a slight back-and-forth twisting motion, into the stem. The shank is normally protected with a silver, gold or horn cap, which adds to the pipe's overall attractiveness. Originally, military bits were designed for British cavalry, most notably those on duty in India, who had a rakish habit of keeping their briars tucked into their belts, like a sword. Unfortunately, this led to a number of serious battlefield pipe casualties, as a quick movement in the saddle or a less-than-perfect dismount and snap! Another briar bites the dust. The military bit provided the perfect solution, as it made it possible for a soldier to instantly pull the pipe apart, placing the bit and bowl into a pocket, safe from harm. It could just as quickly be reassembled for a smoke.

These bits are just as practical today. The main thing to guard against is a military bit that fits too loosely or that has not been shoved down firmly. I remember a meeting I had in the office of a V.I.P. (Very Important Pipesmoker). I was smoking a gold spigot military bit Peterson at the time. As the fellow turned to answer his phone, the bowl of my pipe dropped into my lap, burning ashes and all. I jumped up out of my chair, repeatedly tossing the bowl into the air and catching it with my hand, like some deranged juggler. I then shoved the bowl back onto my pipe, leaned against the wall and kept on puffing as if nothing had happened.

My friend, suddenly aware of my gyrations, looked up in surprise.

"Are you going somewhere?" he asked. His secretary was laughing so hard she had to leave the room.

An important decision is to decide whether or not to buy a pipe that uses a filter. Filters are interesting devices that allegedly trap the nicotine, tars and juices from the tobacco before they reach your mouth. Some, like the 9mm and more recent 6mm charcoal and meerschaum filters that are inserted in the specially constructed mouthpieces, work quite well. Others, like the metal filters that were popular in

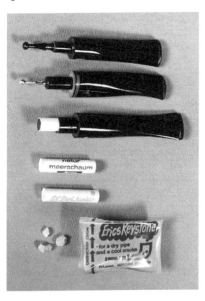

There are various styles of pipe filters (top to bottom): two versions of metal filters, replaceable 9mm filters of either charcoal or meerschaum (6mm filters are also available for pipes with thinner shanks), and absorbent particles, such as Erics Keystones (also meerschaum and clay), that are dropped into the bowl before filling it with tobacco.

The Peterson system is also a filter pipe of sorts, as the hollowed-out "reservoir" helps trap foul-tasting tobacco juices. Shown above the cut-away model are a rusticated pipe with nickel cap, and a gold spigot.

the 1930s and are still in use today in some pipes, are less than effective and only succeed in condensing the tars and juices in the pipe, thereby creating a pool of rancid liquid and preventing the use of a pipe cleaner. Whether or not to buy a filter pipe is a very controversial topic.

Most American pipesmokers disapprove of filters, metal, charcoal, or otherwise, believing that they taint the pure flavor of the tobacco smoke, which must pass through the impurities compounded in the filter before it reaches your taste buds. Only the cheapest pipes in America have filters. Yet, by comparison, just the opposite is true in Germany, where over 90% of all pipes sold are of the filter type. So important is the German filter market that companies like Stanwell make special filter pipes just for Germany and the Vauen pipe company owes a great deal of its success to the popularity of its Dr. Perl disposable filters, of which they sell three million a week! GBD and Comoy's also make filter pipes especially for the German pipesmoker and both Stanwell and Duncan replaceable charcoal filters are extremely popular items. Although most Italians do not smoke filter pipes, they cannot ignore its existence, and so Savinelli has its balsa system and Don Carlos has come out with its Hydra dry smoking filter pipe. In addition, the London-made Kaywoodie and the popular Falcon are just two popular pipes that feature metal

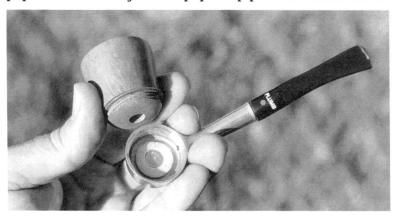

Some pipes incorporate a filter as part of their overall design, such as the Dr. Plumb Peacemaker, which ceased production in 1985 but has now been brought back. It features interchangeable bowls, a replaceable absorbent filter ring, and an aluminum body for strength and easy cleaning. The flat-bottomed pipe is easy to stand up.

filters and the British have just reintroduced the Dr. Plumb Peacemaker, a pipe with an absorbent filter ring and a removable bowl.

Still, most of the high-grade pipemakers do not put filters of any kind in their pipes, believing they are unnecessary and adversely affect the taste of the tobacco. From a design standpoint, a filter also requires a thicker shank, thereby making for a less graceful looking pipe. True, Alfred Dunhill puts its 1912-era "inner tube" metallic filter in every one of its pipes, but this is a bit of nostalgia at best. Practically every Alfred Dunhill pipesmoker removes this filter immediately after buying the pipe and certainly before filling it with tobacco. In addition, many connoisseurs of high-grade pipes throughout the world refuse to smoke a filter pipe. Indeed, the filter pipe controversy is far from over and is one of those highly opinionated topics for which there may never be an answer. Personally, I prefer a non-filter pipe and instead, use pipe cleaners whenever my tobacco starts to gurgle or

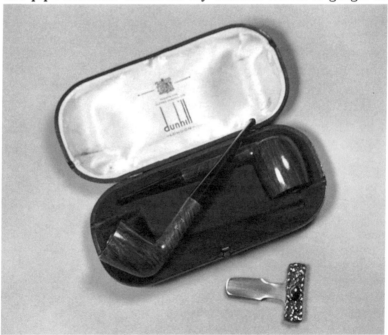

Too rare to smoke? The author thinks not. An extremely desirable factory cased set of Dunhill dead root briars stamped DRRH and made in 1950. The Dunhill pipe reamer is a tiger's eye silver bark finish dating from the 1960s.

Charatan is a popular British brand now being made in France. However, these particular Charatans were made years ago in Britain, are unsmoked, and therefore carry a premium among collectors. (top) An Extra Large egg shape; (bottom) the popular After Hours model, with its original box.

Sasieni is another English pipe no longer being made by the original company. The currently made pipes are quite affordable and represent good value. However, the dots on the older British-made Sasieni's can greatly affect their values. Shown here are the three variations (top to bottom): One-Dot European version (shape 101 XXL patent number), with no British town name used to denote shape; the more readily found Four-Dot "Pembroke" shape with patent number and a natural finish; and an early Eight-Dot "Felsted" natural finish patent number.

taste a little bitter, as discussed in Chapter 3. This instantly produces a clean, dry smoke.

There is another pipe buying trend that you should be aware of, although for now it is primarily an American phenomena. However, I have already seen evidence of it spreading to Germany as well as England and parts of Italy. It is the hobby of collecting and smoking "estate pipes," that is, vintage pipes made of old briar or carved in shapes that are no longer available or made by companies that are no longer in business. Like buying a vintage automobile that has been restored, these previously-smoked pipes have been sterilized inside with boiling alcohol, cleaned and polished outside, with special care being taken not to change the original finish or any of the stamped nomenclature, all of which affects the pipe's value.

Admittedly, there is something unsettling about smoking a pipe that someone else once owned, but in reality, it is no different than eating with silverware at a restaurant. We know we are not the first to use that knife and fork, but it doesn't concern us because they have been cleaned and sterilized. It is the same concept with estate pipes. Why

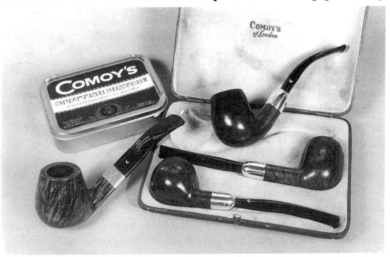

Comoy's are both collectable and smokable: (L) The initial 1997 offering of the Explorer Series, featuring 150 individually numbered, silver banded pipes saluting Sir Francis Drake; and (R) a rare factory cased set of matching silver mounted Blue Ribands from the 1940s, shown with an unopened tin of no-longer-produced Comoy's tobacco.

would anyone want an old pipe when he could buy a new one you ask? Well first, not just any used pipe is an estate pipe. To be desirable, it must be a brand that people want, like Dunhill or any of the older Charatans and Barlings, to give just three examples. Secondly, only estate pipes made with exceptional wood are collectable, such as a Dunhill straight grain stamped DR (for Dead Root) or a Comoy's straight grain Blue Riband. Many of these older pipes were made with exceptionally old Algerian briar, which is basically unobtainable today. So much of estate pipe collecting is motivated by the lure of having something that is no longer available. And finally, there is the matter of price, for estate pipes normally sell for about half the cost of a new pipe. There are exceptions, of course, and a particularly desirable pipe, such a cased pair of Dunhills from the 1950s might fetch thousands of dollars at a pipe show, where 20th century briars are displayed on tables by their owners and sold or traded to other collectors. Although estate pipe collecting isn't for everyone, it is a growing trend that you should know about. (For more infor-

Christmas, electric trains, and pipes are an American tradition. Image this toy train trilogy under your tree: (L to R) an S&R Woodcrafts diamond-shanked bulldog by Steve and Roswetha Anderson; a fantastically grained natural briar by Clarence Mickles, featuring an antique gold band; and a limited edition Hand Made Freehand by Kaywoodie. The train is the E6 Atlantic by Lionel, an O gauge locomotive that features digital sounds and prototypical details.

mation, read my book, *Rare Smoke — The Ultimate Guide To Pipe Collecting.*)

When in doubt as to which pipe to select, buy a respected brand name. My personal technique — which I have to admit drives some people crazy but it does work — is to line up all of the pipes that I think I might want on the counter in front of me. Then I inspect each one carefully, noting its design, workmanship and cost. One by one, I eliminate the pipes I don't want, until I am left with the finalist. That is the pipe I end up buying. If the shop has a mirror, stand in front of it with each of the various pipes you are considering, to see how they look next to your face. After all, like a custom made suit, a pipe must not only look good, it must make you look good!

Remember, you can never have too many pipes. I have some for elegant evenings on the town, some for staying at home by the fireplace, some for making public appearances as a speaker, and some for no other reason other than the fact

Today, pipesmoking is enjoying a rediscovery throughout the world. In America, pipe buying shows like this one are extremely popular, attracting hobbyists from all over the world to smoke, exhibit, sell, and trade pipes with one another. These "pipe expo's" are now starting to occur in other countries as well.

that I like them. Like shirts and ties and hats, you should have a pipe for every conceivable occasion.

For me, one of the most personal tributes to picking the right pipe was portrayed by my late friend, Jeremy Brett, the actor who so convincingly embodied the spirit of Sherlock Holmes for Granada Television. In *The Return of Sherlock Holmes* story entitled, "The Adventure of the Empty House," there is a scene, near the end of that episode, when Jeremy picks two pipes up from the mantle. One is the Peterson churchwarden that he smoked throughout his previous Sherlock Holmes series. The other is a custom pipe that I designed and had made for him. In a twinkling he puts the Peterson aside and lights up the pipe that I gave him. He knew I would catch the significance. It was a great tribute by a great actor to the real meaning of picking the right pipe.

Of course, the internet is changing the way pipe buying is being done in the 21st century. It is now possible to surf the web for the briar of your dreams. But your computer screen cannot tell you how a pipe feels in your hands nor reveal how well it is made. Only physical contact can do that, so if buying a pipe from a dealer or an individual on the internet, be sure you have return privileges, the same that you would get from a tobacconist if you bought a pipe and then wanted to exchange it, unsmoked, for another brand or style.

Still there is nothing like the experience of buying your pipe from a knowledgeable tobacconist. (Just make sure that the person standing behind the counter is a pipesmoker, otherwise he has no business being there as he cannot possibly empathize with your needs.) The anticipation of what you might find just by entering a well stocked pipe store is half of the fun — one of the last great civilized adventures. It is like walking into a pipe club meeting, full of comrades with a similar interest, jovial conversation and the wonderful fragrance of pipe smoke. And creating a pleasant aura of pipe smoke is what the next chapter is all about.

There's nothing like an after-dinner Hookah, as the author
demonstrates at Neyla, a Middle Eastern/American restaurant in the MGM Grand in Las Vegas. After a hearty feast
of petite mezza, lacquered duck, and rose blossom crème
brûlée, a water pipe will be brought to any reader of this
book who asks for it.

photo: Joan P. Hacker

Chapter 3
THE PIPESMOKING RITUAL

Ever since the first pipe was put between a smoker's lips, one of the great mysteries of "civilized" society has been how to smoke a pipe without having your tongue bite the mouth that feeds it. Indeed, "tongue bite," that sharp, painful burning sensation all too common with many neophyte puffers, is one of the chief reasons most people give up pipesmoking after only a few unsuccessful tries. No doubt they are left with the belief that all tobaccophiles are confirmed masochists who, in addition to smoking a pipe, also take pleasure in putting heavy starch in their underwear. But the reality is, tongue bite is not a part of normal pipesmoking at all. Unfortunately, few new pipesmokers are properly instructed on how to smoke a pipe. This one glaring omission is the main reason so many potential pipe people turn away from their briars before they have even started to put a decent cake on them.

Smoking a pipe is an art form derived from skills, and like most skills, it cannot be fully appreciated until you have mastered the technique. Happily, anyone can learn them and the proof of that statement is best typified by the author himself, having come from a non-smoking family. When I lit up my very first briar which I randomly crammed with a fistful of nondescript tobacco, there were no veteran pipeologists standing nearby to tell me what I was or was not doing correctly. Inasmuch as practical "how-to" pipe books always have been relatively scarce, I learned from experience. One of the many pleasures I hope you will derive from these pages are some of those smoke shrouded pipe-puffing secrets, which I now gladly share with you.

Tongue bite is caused by one of three things: 1) a pipe that has not been properly "broken in"; 2) incorrectly packing the pipe with tobacco; and 3) trying to smoke tobacco that is not properly humidified.

Compounding the tongue bite problem is the fact that many new pipesmokers are multi-pack-a-day cigarette smokers, and turn to a briar either on their doctor's orders (a fairly common prescription, given to break them of the nicotine habit and generally, far more effective than nicotine patches or gum) or out of their own desire to free themselves from an uncontrollable addiction and turn it into a controllable pleasure. It is important to realize that pipesmoking is not like cigarette smoking, a fact that I have a hard time convincing anti-smoking news reporters to accept. In any case, one of the most difficult things a cigarette smoker will have to do is not so much give up "the weed," but rather, to learn how to properly smoke a pipe, as all the old cigarette smoking habits must be overcome.

For one thing, pipesmokers do not inhale; to do so defeats the very essence of pipesmoking, which is to "taste" the tobacco in your mouth, just as if you were tasting a wine. Inhaling pure, untainted pipe smoke into the lungs is like gargling with a fine 1994 vintage Cabernet Sauvignon. Not only is it uncouth and ignorant, but you will never be able to fully appreciate the natural flavor of the tobacco and the relaxing benefits of the pipe. Besides, pipe tobacco is much purer and richer than anything cigarette paper was ever wrapped around, but because the smoke is not drawn into your lungs, you do not absorb large concentrations of nicotine into your bloodstream, which is one of the reasons pipesmoking is not physically addictive.

In addition to the health and psychological benefits of pipesmoking, the cigarette smoker should also consider the economic advantages: while it might take an average cigarette smoker about ten minutes to nervously go through a single cigarette, the average pipesmoker, using a medium-sized bowl, can easily puff away for 30 to 45 minutes. Considering the fact that there are about 30 to 40 pipefuls of tobacco in every 50 gram package (with a slight variance being allowed for pipe bowl size and the cut of the tobacco itself), pipesmoking represents one of the greatest values of our modern-day society, even with its shockingly high taxes that the government insists on levying as punishment on its most law-abiding citizens.

For the fullest measure of enjoyment, it should be remembered that a pipe is sipped, like a fine cognac. In this way, the full, rich smoke is drawn into the mouth, held there briefly as the flavor is sensed, then gently exhaled in a white, scented cloud. An interesting sidelight to this is the fact that the pipesmoker cannot smell the aroma of his tobacco; only those around him have access to that olfactory pleasure. For years, I have heard others comment on the rather pungent odor of the strong English blends I smoke, but I could never really identify with their statements until the day I put my pipe in an ashtray while I went outside for a few minutes to check on the sunset. When I returned, the house was filled with a rich, heavy fragrance reminiscent of autumn nights, campfires, forests, and hunting lodges. It was the tobacco aroma from my own pipe, which I was smelling for the first time.

Moderation is an important key to truly enjoyable pipesmoking; an overindulgence in anything pleasurable takes away from its benefits, often with very unpleasant side effects. A bottle of 1990 Dom Perignon — one of the greatest champagne vintages of the 20th century — can be a very elegant treat reserved for a special occasion, but quaff down six or seven of those costly corkages and no longer are the senses able to comprehend the qualities of that fine bubbly. Instead, you are left with a painful, brain-throbbing reminder of your overindulgence the next morning. The same is true with pipe tobacco. Each smoker has a limit as to how many bowlfuls his or her body will tolerate. The daily temperament

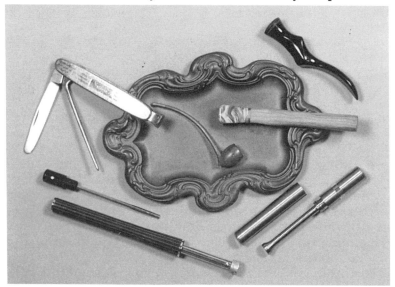

Pipe tampers are one of the most important accessories you can own. (clockwise from upper left:) British-made Rogers pipe tool; Nørding acrylic and brass tamper; Georg Jensen "match" tamper; Davidoff titanium and gold pipe tool; Vauen's retractable tamper from Germany.

of each individual also affects this tolerance level, and I have found that I will smoke more bowlfuls of tobacco when busy or under pressure (no doubt subconsciously using the pipe to help me relax) than I will when my Ship of Life is cruising in calmer waters.

Smoking habits can also be affected by our surroundings. For example, I rarely have the proverbial "morning pipe" unless it is a special occasion, like the first day of vacation or Christmas Day. Ordinarily I smoke my pipe in the late afternoon or the evening. However, years ago when I worked in a corporate office where a number of my fellow executives were also pipesmokers (the fact that we had the freedom to smoke where we worked will tell you how long ago that was), we would all find ourselves lighting up by mid-morning, smoking through the lunch hour and into the late afternoon. The constant aroma of someone else's pipe tobacco and the sight of others contentedly puffing away in meetings or while on the phone was too much to resist; we each had to get in there and partake of our common enjoyment. But even then, my body would tell me when to slow down, for unlike cigarette smoking, one doesn't always "need" a pipe. It should be enjoyed as a hobby, not a habit.

The art of pipesmoking begins properly enough, by filling the pipe with tobacco. Now, as uncomplicated as that may sound, it actually is the single most important step in maximizing the enjoyment from your pipe. And, if done correctly, is one of the "secret ingredients" that will not only help eliminate tongue bite, but will also enable your pipe to stay lit longer with fewer matches.

Ever since pipesmokers learned they could puff and write at the same time, there have been innumerable theories, techniques and treatises done, redone, and redundant on the correct methods of packing a pipe. Some techniques were written by people who obviously were not pipesmokers at all, while other methods only worked part of the time, depending on the tobacco, the mental condition of the smoker, and even, I suspect, the phase of the moon. The pipe-filling technique I am about to give you has continuously worked for me in scores of pipes and throughout a period that has encompassed decades. Moreover, ever since I first described it in one of my books, it has become a technique taught by many tobacconists to first-time purchasers of pipes, realizing that a satisfied pipesmoker is also a satisfied customer.

First, check to make sure your pipe is completely clear of foreign matter. That means no left-over bits of tobacco in the airhole from the last smoke, and no gray ash in the bowl. Besides a visual check, it also helps to gently blow through the mouthpiece of the pipe to make sure there is nothing lodged inside the stem that could impede the flow of air. I once had a frustrating bout trying to light a large briar calabash before I realized that there was a pipe cleaner hidden within its unusually long curved shank. Trying to puff under these conditions does put color into your cheeks!

If your pipe is a brand new, never-before-smoked briar, it is a good idea to rub a very thin coating of honey around the inside of the bowl with your finger, making sure you completely cover the heel and side walls, but take care to keep the sticky stuff off the outside wood. The honey on the inside of the bowl speeds up the process of building a "cake," or thick charred coating in your pipe bowl, another one of the factors that will help eliminate tongue bite. A properly built-up cake will also keep your pipesmoking cooler and will enable you to derive the fullest flavor from your tobacco. This cake serves as both a fireplace-type grate and an insulator for the pipe bowl. Normally, it will take about five to seven bowlfuls to begin building an adequate cake.

Personally, I happen to enjoy breaking in a new pipe. It is like meeting a friend for the first time and getting to know one another as we smoke. There is a definite sense of adventure in being the very first to load the bowl, tamp the tobacco, light the leaves and take a puff, drawing the thick white smoke through the untouched stem much as an explorer blazes a new path through an uncharted land.

I once had a college friend who so enjoyed smoking new pipes that he would offer to break in briars for anyone in our crowd. In about a week's time he would give them back a cleaned and sterilized pipe with a healthy cake built up within its bowl. For many pipesmokers, breaking in a new briar is a necessary evil and I often thought my school chum could have made a decent living by charging money for his break-in services.

But breaking in someone's pipe for them isn't a new idea. Back in the 1940s, the well-known pipe London pipe shop of Astleys would, upon request, put a customer's newly-purchased pipe in a special smoking bellows that would gently puff away with their favorite blend for about three days, or until the customer returned to pick up his briar. So if you purchased a pipe at Astleys on Saturday and came to pick it up the following weekend, it would have a nice newly formed cake, ready to smoke.

Breaking in a pipe, whether done mechanically or "in person," is a very important process in preparing your briar for a lifetime of smoking enjoyment and is not something that should be rushed. I learned this the hard way. Back during my earliest pipesmoking days in college, I conducted a unique experiment involving trying to get an instant cake on a pipe. I had not yet discovered there were pipes other than the cheap drugstore variety and I had grown disgusted with the harsh bitter taste of the breaking-in process I had experienced with the two pipes I already owned. Therefore, upon purchasing yet another heavily lacquered, red colored pipe (it wasn't so much that I was a slow learner — it was just that in those days I didn't know any better and obviously, I did not have this book to read), I packed my new briar full of a coarse Burley tobacco, fired it up with a packet of paper matches, climbed into my 1954 Austin-Healey four-banger and roared down the highway for about an hour holding my redhot glowing pipe out the window to "properly" break it in within a record time. At 70 miles an hour the smoke was pouring out of the mouthpiece like a steam engine! At the end of my experiment I confidently brought the pipe back into the roadster and looked at what I expected would be a nice charred, evenly caked bowl. Instead, the pipe looked like it had been created in Dr. Frankenstein's lab; the entire exterior finish was bubbled and cracked and the bowl had burnt completely through at the heel. At three dollars for the pipe and ten cents for a packet of tobacco it was a relatively inexpensive lesson, but it taught me something I never forgot: to this day I will not smoke a pipe in an Austin-Healey.

Some new pipes come with their bowls already precarbonized as an aid to cake-building, but even these should have a thin honey coating to help with those first few all-important bowls of tobacco. However, this honey-coating should only be applied to briar pipes; it is not needed in clay pipes (which are absorbent and will season of their own accord without building a cake) and should definitely never be applied to meerschaum or meerschaum-lined pipes, as the build-up of a cake in these porous bowls is not desirable, for it separates the tobacco from the meerschaum and will impede the coloring process, thereby defeating the unique benefits of meerschaum as a pipesmoking material. Likewise, honey should not be used in the porous corncob unless you plan on eating it.

Of course, a briar pipe that has been properly"broken in" will already have this cake, which should never be allowed to get any thicker than a nickel (about ⅟₁₆ of an inch), otherwise there is a danger of it becoming so thickly encrusted it will expand when hot and crack your pipe bowl. Additionally, an overly thick cake means your pipe will hold less tobacco. Your tobacconist can show you a variety of special adjustable reaming tools that can be used to keep the cake trimmed down to the proper thickness. Some people opt to keep their cake trimmed with a common pocket knife, but pointed blades run the risk of piercing the cake and cutting into the briar, and are ill-suited for getting an even trim all the way around the bowl. So do your pipe a favor; spend a couple of extra dollars and get a proper reamer.

With your pipe empty and clean, it is time to add that most precious of ingredients, tobacco. In Chapter 4, we will be discussing the various types of *Nicotiana Tabacum* available, but for now, suffice to say pipe tobacco generally comes in one of two basic forms: caked (pressed tightly together) or loose (much more common and encountered with house blends from tobacconists or when buying most pre-packaged tobaccos in foil pouches or tins). Either way, before filling your pipe, the tobacco must be carefully broken up and separated so that no solid clumps will impede the flow of air necessary to keep the tobacco burning. Even tobacco that is finely cut, such as Virginia, or the last vestiges of a long leaf English blend that have been sitting on the bottom of your humidor, will occasionally have a tendency to "lock leaves," and should be gently separated with the fingers before it enters the hallowed region of your pipe bowl.

The pipe-filling procedure must actually be repeated three times in order to properly pack a single bowlful of tobacco. First, take a pinch of tobacco in your fingers and trickle it into your pipe until the bowl is loosely filled and completely full, almost to overflowing. Then, gently tap the side of the bowl to settle the leaves of tobacco against one another. Visibly, you may notice the level of the tobacco lowering ever so slightly. This is good. Next, using your finger or a pipe tamper (whichever is handier), gently press the tobacco further into the bowl until it feels slightly springy. Normally, this will compress the tobacco so that it fills the bottom third of the bowl. Repeat this tobacco-filling process a second time, pressing down slightly firmer, which should now bring the tobacco to about one-third from the top of the

The Pipe-Lighting Ritual

First, run a pipe cleaner through the pipe to make sure the airhole is clear.

Trickle in enough tobacco to fill the pipe and gently tap side of bowl with fingers to settle the tobacco to the bottom. Do this three times, or until the bowl is full.

Gently press the tobacco down so that it feels "springy" but not hard.

With a wooden match or butane lighter, slowly "walk" the flame around the tobacco, while puffing slowly. This is the charring light.

The burnt tobacco will "rise" in the bowl. Gently tamp the tobacco down below the bowl rim.

Light up again, puffing slowly and rhythmically. Then sit back and relax with an old friend...this is the best part!

bowl. Finally, gravity-feed tobacco into your pipe bowl for the third time, filling it to overflowing and press down on the load firmly, so that the tobacco is now even with the top of the pipe bowl. Be sure to retain that "springy" feeling in your tobacco. Otherwise, you may be pressing down too hard and by compressing the tobacco too tightly you may make it difficult or even impossible to keep your pipe lit. When this happens, it is best to empty everything out of the bowl and start over.

It is important that you only pack a pipe with fresh, humidified tobacco, as dry tobacco will crunch down and produce a hot and quick burning smoke, which immediately translates into tongue bite. When filling your pipe, it's a good practice to occasionally draw some air through the mouthpiece, to make sure you are not packing your tobacco too tightly and to insure that the airhole has not become plugged with a tiny chunk of tobacco. The correct tobacco-filling procedure takes a little practice, but after a few times you will automatically develop this all- important skill and will be able to actually "feel" when you have a properly filled pipe.

You can't smoke your pipe without a light, and here are some of the best: (L to R) DuPont leather and gold Gatsby; Sillem sterling silver matching lighter and tamper; gold Dunhill Unique; Corona 90 degree pipe lighter with embossed pipe shape chart and a Corona 90 degree lighter in gold, both with retractable tamper. The antique Doulton Lambeth match holder in the background is from England.

We are now ready to light up, thereby inaugurating our potential pleasure with a baptism by fire. For this all-important act, use only wooden matches or a butane (gas) flame lighter. Paper matches are impregnated with chemicals that will taint the tobacco and its taste, as will lighter fluid. Wooden matches and butane have no such impurities and burn "clean." However, when using wooden matches, pause a second after striking the match, so that the sulfur will burn off . Otherwise, you will get a bitter mouthful of sulfur smoke mixed in with your tobacco smoke. When using gas, be aware that a butane flame burns hotter than a wooden match, and therefore, care must be taken to avoid charring the rim of your pipe bowl during the lighting process. And by all means, stay away from those supercharged blowtorch-type butane lighters that are such crowd-pleasers when firing up your cigar. Their 2400 F degree pinpoint flame is far too hot for briar and can sear its way right through your prized Dunhill quicker than an intergalactic star warrior's solar ray. Save these hand blasters for welding, which, by the way, is what they were originally designed for.

Pipe lighting is a two-part procedure. The first step is called the *false* or *charring* light. Its purpose is to create a charred "lid" completely covering the top of your bowlful of tobacco, thereby making a "fire platform" which will permit your carefully packed pipe to smoke evenly all they way down to the bottom or heel of the bowl. To begin the charring light, move the flame from your lighter or match slowly over the entire area of the tobacco, taking care not to scorch the edges of the pipe — it may discolor soon enough of its own accord after a number of repeated smokes. Try to keep this disfiguration to a minimum, as it will affect not only the beauty, but the value of your pipe. As you light the tobacco, draw in on your pipe with long, smooth puffs, thereby sucking the flame down into the tobacco. When the entire top surface of the tobacco has been completely and evenly lit, take the pipe from your mouth and gently press down on the ashes with a pipe tamper (the ashes will rise above the rim of the bowl during the charring light), pushing them down upon the unburned tobacco underneath.

Now you are ready for your second light. Once again, "walk" the flame over the entire area of the now-charred tobacco as you puff slowly and rhythmically. That's all there is to it. Besides giving you a better smoke, these step-by-step pipe lighting techniques can give you a decided advantage during an argument. For example, if you are starting to lose a debate with your opponent, pause from the encounter to fill, light, and tamp your pipe (furthering the popular conjecture that pipesmokers are deep, philosophical thinkers). Then, as the first clouds of gray haze lift from your briar and your antagonist is starting to feel a bit uneasy because of the lull, look him squarely in the eye, slowly take the pipe from your mouth and overwhelm him with the profound retort you have had ample time to conjure up.

Your pipe will stay lit longer if you periodically keep the ashes tamped down upon the remaining tobacco and if you gently blow a whisper of air into the stem occasionally; your breath acts like a miniature bellows to keep the tobacco burning. That is why pipesmokers who talk with their pipes in their mouths require fewer matches to keep their briars lit; the breath from their speech helps keep the glow alive. That's also why pipesmokers are so adept at heated discussions.

As you smoke your pipe, moisture will invariably accumulate in the bottom of the bowl and within the stem. Sometimes this is evidenced by an annoying gurgling sound. This liquid is caused by the burning of the tobacco, for one of the by-products of combustion is moisture. Compounding the situation, some tobaccos — most noticeably aromatics — burn "wetter" than others (more about this in Chapter 4). In addition, some individuals smoke wetter than others and it is not uncommon for saliva to invariably mix with these tart tobacco liquids. The result is a sudden acidic taste as these juices are drawn into the smoke and often into your mouth. This moisture must be removed from the pipe before enjoyable puffing can continue. Sometimes this liquid can be adequately absorbed by a disposable filter. But for non-filter pipes, the easiest solution is to run a pipe cleaner through the mouthpiece and into the bowl to soak up the juices. If you can't get a pipe cleaner to go all the way into the pipe (a common malady, especially with bents), here is a hint: Before inserting the pipe cleaner, put a slight bend on the end. When resistance is felt in the pipe, back the pipe cleaner out ever so slightly, twist it to rearrange the bend, and push the cleaner back into the pipe again. By rotating the cleaner and "feeling" your way through the airhole, you will usually get through. Sometimes this procedure can be a little frustrating, but do not attempt to remove the shank while the pipe is still hot, or you could crack the pipe.

Of course, once you get the soggy pipe cleaner out of the pipe, what do you do with it? The etiquette of using a pipe cleaner in mixed company is a somewhat unpleasant experience: the pipe cleaner comes out looking rather dark and smelling quite rank. Therefore, if I'm with a group of people and my pipe starts misbehaving, I will excuse myself and venture off to some unobserved area to perform this brief pipe cleaning act in private. If in a car, business meeting or similar enclosed environment where I cannot get away, I will simply insert a pipe cleaner to soak up the juices and keep them from permeating the briar. Then I let my pipe rest until it can be cleaned discreetly. However, when in my own den or in the company of fellow pipesmokers, I use pipe cleaners wantonly and with little regard for their preservation. They are an extremely inexpensive means for insuring the continuation of a "clean" smoke. One of the worst situations a pipesmoker can imagine is being stranded on a desert island with ten pounds of choice tobacco, a rack full of high-grade briars...and no pipe cleaners!

Used pipe cleaners are rather smelly and are best disposed of in the fireplace or hidden deep within the darkest confines of a garbage bag away from the house. Their odor can bring out the worst in people. I remember taking a flight from New York to Los Angeles a few years ago. Of course, it was a non-smoking airline, as all of them are in America. Now, the United States is a big country; it takes five hours to fly from New York to Los Angeles. As I had already seen the in-flight movie, I thought I would make use of the time by cleaning my pipes, which I always pack in my carry-on luggage to avoid breakage. I lowered my tray table, and spread out all of my briars, plus my reamer and pipe cleaners. I didn't think anyone would object to such a harmless activity. Well, by the time I got to my second bent bulldog, two women sitting across the aisle from me did. And very vocally, too. It was obvious they were not pipesmokers. I was finally asked by a rather indignant flight attendant to put away all of my toys. So now we know that not only are these non-smoking flights, they are also non-pipe cleaning flights. The moral of this story is: Nobody appreciates a used pipe cleaner, whether on the ground or 34,000 feet in the air.

It is important to remember that any pipe will go out if left unattended. In fact, no matter how well you've packed it, no matter how thoroughly you've lit it, all pipes require additional lightings before the entire bowlful is consumed. That is part of the joy and relaxation of pipesmoking: the frequent lightings and re-lightings and watching the billowing clouds of smoke playfully rise and stumble over each other until, exhausted, they finally disperse across the room.

An average pipeful of tobacco usually lasts from thirty to forty-five minutes, depending upon the size of the pipe bowl and the intensity of the puffing. During that time I have used as little as three and as many as twelve matches just to keep my briar alive and well. Of course, many pipesmokers pride themselves on only using one match to keep an entire bowl burning right on down to the last gram of tobacco. In fact, ever since 1723 there have been pipesmoking contests to determine who can keep a bowlful of pre-measured tobacco (historically 3.3 grams of Burley cube) going the longest, using only two wooden matches. Back when I was officiating at some of these pipesmoking contests, I used to call them "the slowest race in the world." They are still held annually throughout the United States, Canada, Europe and Japan.

Personally, I do not want to be competitive when smoking my pipe. Just the opposite. I am competitive enough in my daily life. I smoke a pipe to relax and forget about the world. Therefore, when smoking for pleasure there are no rules and I can use as many matches as I wish. So do not be surprised that, in the course of smoking a bowlful of tobacco, you too will undoubtedly have to re-light your pipe numerous times. Unlike cigarettes, which smoke stronger each time they are relit, it is one of the phenomena of pipe tobacco that the taste will not be materially affected by continual relighting after it has gone out, as long as you relight before the ash grows cold. I have even relit a pipe that has gone out for a couple of hours, with no ill effects. However, if you let a half-smoked pipe sit overnight and then try to smoke it the next day, it will be bitter and harsh. And so will you.

No matter how many matches you use, no matter how often you tamp, and however long it takes to consume the contents of your bowl, the primary objective, especially with a new pipe, is to smoke all the tobacco, right down to the heel, for that is the only way to build up a perfect cake, thereby insuring many memorable smokes for you and your briar in the years ahead. All too often, one encounters an otherwise well-smoked pipe that has a perfect cake built up around the upper part of the bowl, but not on the bottom. It is the telltale sign of the "incomplete smoker," an unfortunate soul who has failed to procure the very last vestiges of pleasure from his pipe.

Here are a few more smoking hints: when a pipe gets too hot to hold or to press against your cheek without burning your skin, you have been smoking it too hard or too fast. The best thing to do is to put it down in an ashtray and let it cool off before relighting and puffing again. I once put a hot pipe down for about fifteen minutes and then picked it up and was able to start smoking it again without relighting, so I *know* it had been burning hot! Additionally, by leaving a layer of ash in your pipe instead of fluffing it out every time you tamp the tobacco down, your pipe will burn a little cooler. However, I never worry about this too much unless I am smoking out-of-doors, where even the gentlest breezes can cause your tobacco to burn hotter than when smoking indoors.

To be sure, smoking in the wind can create its own set of problems by causing your pipe to burn hot and can actually ruin a new pipe that hasn't been properly caked. One of the reasons briar is the most desirable wood for a pipe is that it is porous (can breathe) yet is hard, which means it will char without burning. However, it still is wood and too hot a temperature within the bowl can cause a burn-out. The end result is a blackened hole in your pipe. Burn-out is caused by one of two reasons: puffing too fast on a brand new pipe or by having a briar pipe with a hidden flaw in the bowl. This soft spot will usually burn before it chars. On a brand new pipe, most responsible tobacconists will replace a burned-out flaw with another pipe as long as you originally purchased the first briar from them and did not abuse it. If the tobacconist won't replace a faulty pipe, then the factory certainly should. Pipe firms are usually a reputable lot and are truly embarrassed by any imperfection found in their product, even when it is Mother Nature, and not their workers, who is the culprit.

Burn-out can also be caused by smoking a pipe in a high wind or an open top convertible. Some companies, such as Peterson, Brebbia, Comoy's, and Alfred Dunhill, make pipes with metal ventilated lids which fit over the bowl to shield it from the wind, yet which provide enough ventilation to keep the pipe burning. It is a design idea that harkens back to the old Germanic Tyrolean pipes. Of course, there is nothing wrong with smoking a pipe in a car with an open sun roof, as the wind never hits the pipe directly and the pipe smoke is immediately aerated from the car interior. But as a safety reminder, don't attempt to light or tamp your pipe while trying to pass that slow-moving Corvette on a winding mountain road.

It is important to remember that you can be serious about your pipesmoking just as long as you do not take your pipesmoking too seriously. It is a pleasurable pastime, not a regulated vocation. Your pipe should provide enjoyment, not frustration. This is not only a physical attribute, but a visual one as well. There is nothing more captivating than to gaze at the polished sheen on the bowl as a pipe is smoked. This gloss is put there by wax, which of course heats and melts deeper into the pores of the wood as the pipe is smoked. I often hold a new pipe by its stem for the first few minutes of the initial smoke, just to watch this shine deepen as the pipe grows warmer. Eventually, however, like shaking hands with a friend for the first time, I grasp the bowl and hold it the way a pipe is normally held. This almost immediately dulls the shine, but a newer finish starts to take hold, one that will eventually transform into the rich, time-worn patina of a well smoked, aged briar that has stood sentinel with your thoughts throughout the years.

Of course, the original wax polish can be resurrected simply by applying carnauba wax to the pipe and buffing it with a soft cloth or a chamois. But it is the older-looking antiqued luster that makes most briars look the richest. This finish can even be accentuated by rubbing the warm pipe against the sides of your nose around the nostrils, and along your forehead — places where a large concentration of natural body oils occur. These oils can then be rubbed with the fingers into the pipe as you smoke it, imparting a deep mellow tone to the wood. In this way, you and your briar start to become as one.

Sadly, however, all good things must come to an end and so it is with our bowlful of tobacco. Eventually, sometimes with much reluctance, other times suddenly with nary a struggle, the glowing bits of tobacco will fade, the embers will die, and a final curl of gray smoke will drift up and away, severing itself for all time from the very pipe that contained its life. Thus, our repast with Lady Tabacum will be over for a while. Only the fading warmth of the bowl in our hand will be left as a brief reminder of our latest encounter with one of life's simplest yet greatest pleasures. But then, this only sets the stage for a whole new ritual, that of caring for your pipe once its service is temporarily ended, much as a sportsman cares for his prized hunting dog after a rewarding day in the fields.

To be sure, there are some smokers who disdain the "chore" (their word, not mine) of cleaning their pipes, almost

The Mastro de Paja "Pasaro" pipe of the year for 1998 is a smokable work of art.

Noted American pipe craftsman Michael Butera hand-carved this flawless Royal Classic and even did his own goldsmithing for the band.

Two perfect straight grains by two pipe carving perfectionists: (top) a briar accented with boxwood by Jess Chonowitsch from Denmark, and (bottom) a graceful oil-cured briar by Karl-Heinz Joura from Germany.

Italian Pipes To Go With Italian Wines (top to bottom): An early collectable Castello Old Antiquari "Egg" shape #93 with two-tone finish, a Don Carlos "One Note" with a smooth finish, and a Brebbia Grand Designer series by Rainer Barbi. The wines are a Colvecchio 1995 Syrah from Tuscany, and a 1996 Lupicaia, a Tenuta del Terricio estate bottled super-Tuscan blend of Cabernet Sauvignon and Merlot aged for 18 months in French oak.

A stunning sculpted freeform design by American pipecarver Randy Wiley, photographed at the Tsankawi Prehistoric Site, an ancient Pueblo Indian reservation at the Bandelier National Monument in New Mexico.

Julius Vesz of Canada carved this exclusive Raindrop shape (the shank emerges from the top of the bowl) from a 200-year-old Calabrian dead root burl. The copper and gold band is from a 19th century German meerschaum and was acquired from a family that created pipes for the Kaiser. The bit was hand carved from Vienna resin stored for 30 years and saved for this highly unusual and collectable pipe.

as if it were a penance to pay for having had the enjoyment of so gracious a smoke. Yet pipe cleaning can be as rewarding as filling a briar in anticipation of lighting it, for cleaning prepares the pipe for a future meeting between tobacco and flame. Samuel Clemens (aka Mark Twain) summed up the pipe cleaning ritual most eloquently when he wrote, "There is a real sense of pleasure in setting before one's own fire with racks piled about, each briar, clay or meerschaum catching the flickering light in its own way. And there is that feeling of achievement at seeing the racks, some moments later, filled with clean, sweet pipes, each ready and waiting to be filled with a favorite blend."

Clemens knew how to enjoy his pipes, whether he was smoking them or not. In fact, it is rumored that he once turned down a lucrative speaking engagement because it fell on the night he regularly set aside for pipe cleaning.

As necessary as the pipe cleaning process may be, you should not be in too great a hurry to get started. First, you must let your pipe cool down completely. Otherwise, you run the risk of cracking the shank when you try to remove the stem, due to the briar's expansion and contraction caused by the heat from your tobacco. Instead, the first thing to do after you have finished smoking your pipe is to fluff out the loose ashes and moist dottle (those blackened and gooey bits in the heel of the pipe) or gently tap the pipe in the palm of your hand so that the muck falls out. Never rap the pipe against your shoe heel or a hard object, as more pipes are broken this way than by any other means. It looks great in the old time movies but doesn't work in real life, especially with a pipe that you purchased with your own hard-earned money and which is not a studio prop.

Once the pipe is emptied, push a pipe cleaner through the stem so that the end is resting inside the bowl. This will help absorb any residual moisture, which is especially prevalent with aromatic tobaccos. Then temporarily put the pipe away, bowl lower than the mouthpiece, until you are ready to clean it. Never smoke your pipe before it has been cleaned or it will eventually start to taste bitter and will have to be neutralized with a liquid pipe solvent or repeated swabbings with pure grain alcohol. Badly neglected pipes should be taken to a tobacconist who specializes in pipe rejuvenation, where they will literally boil out the bowl with alcohol to bring it back to its original smoking quality.

Older pipes that repeatedly smoke with a sour taste can be neutralized by plugging up the shank, filling the bowl with non-iodine salt, and then putting in 4 to 6 drops of pure grain alcohol. Let the pipe sit overnight, but not for more than eight hours. The salt will turn a dark brown as all of the impurities are leeched out of the bowl. Then carefully scrape out the darkened salt, being careful not to get any on the outside of the pipe, as it can strip the finish. Unplug the shank, wipe out the bowl, and clean the pipe as you normally would. The next bowlful will smoke like a brand new pipe. *But a word of warning:* do not get any salt in the shank or let the alcohol-salt mixture sit for longer than eight hours, or you could dry out the wood to a point where it will crack.

It is advisable to let a recently cleaned pipe air out and dry for at least a day before taking it up again. Most pipe-smokers own more than one pipe and are thus able to smoke a fresh pipe while the last one smoked is "resting." Traditionally, the ideal number of pipes for a smoker to own is seven, the theory being that a different pipe is to be smoked each day of the week, thereby insuring that each pipe will be clean and dry. In fact, there are some very rare matched briar "seven day sets" created by master pipemakers and specially cased just for this purpose. Of course, there is nothing to stop anyone

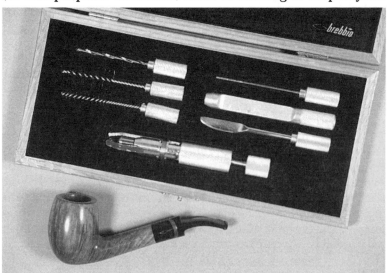

The Brebbia Pipe Service Set keeps all of the specialized tools you'll need for cleaning in one wooden case. It is shown with a Brebbia Linea A straight grain.

from assembling his own "working man's" seven day set made up of any pipes that catch your fancy and pocketbook. Moreover, the commendable goal of always having a fresh pipe to smoke is little enough excuse to go out and buy yourself another new pipe should the mood suddenly strike you.

Personally, I always thought the seven day set theory was a bit unrealistic, for it assumes that pipes are cleaned the day — or at the very worst, no more than six days — after they are smoked. I rarely clean my pipes the day after I've smoked them. In fact, it is often a full month or more before I can settle down and thoroughly clean my pipes with all the loving attention that they deserve. However, as a temporary measure I may fluff out the ashes and run a pipe cleaner through the stem and into the bowl. The fact that I have so little free time is the very rationale I have successfully used to amass a collection of over 2,000 pipes, thereby insuring that I can go through six full years (including Leap Year) before I finally throw another log on the fire on a rainy Saturday afternoon, surround myself with all of my pipe cleaning accoutrements, and, with perhaps my last remaining clean pipe clenched firmly in my teeth, thoroughly immerse myself in the enjoyable task that lies ahead (and in fact all around me). . . bringing my beloved pipes back to life. For me, pipe cleaning is therapeutic.

Here are my pipes — two week's worth —- waiting to be cleaned, with all of the necessary items near at hand.

Like any endeavor of such magnitude, there are certain specialized tools one must have in order to properly perform the pipe cleaning task. Fortunately, none of these items are expensive. First and foremost are pipe cleaners, those elongated fuzzy-coated lengths of wire that are indispensable to the pipesmoker before, after and during his bout with briar or meerschaum. It is a toss-up as to whether a pipesmoker will use more matches or pipe cleaners in his lifetime, but the fact is that pipe cleaners are the smoker's ultimate throwaway. You use them once and into the fireplace they go (the only sure way to get rid of those foul-smelling things, leaving nothing behind but a tell-tale wire strand in the cold gray ashes the next morning).

Pipe cleaners come in three basic styles; the thin and non-tapered absorbent ones, the thick-to-thin tapered absorbent version, and the coarse bristle "Reem 'n Clean" style, not as absorbent as the others and best suited for reaming out coagulated gunk from a badly neglected or hard-smoked pipe. Personally, I use all three; the Reem 'n Cleans are used to scrape out the shank, where most of the gook occurs, the non-tapered absorbents are used for pipes with very thin air holes in their stems and the tapered (my favorites), are used for cleaning the airholes and shanks in larger-bored pipes, swabbing out the bowl of all loose ash, and cramming into the pipe, thick end resting in the bowl after a smoke to let any remaining residue absorb into its fluffy little body overnight. The thicker ends of these tapered cleaners, especially when doubled up and used as a swab, also aid tremendously in absorbing moisture from the heel of pipe bowls and the reservoir cavities of pipes such as the Peterson. Because I go through so many cleaners, I never buy just one package at a time; instead I purchase my pipe cleaners in multiples of ten packages at once. There is no price break, but that gives me 4,500 pipe cleaners and a tremendous feeling of security when lighting up.

In addition to pipe cleaners, you should also have a pipe tool that has a thin, sturdy wire pick to break up bits of caked tobacco or dottle from the heel of the pipe bowl, and a flat miniature shovel-like device for scooping out the residue. Sometimes these inexpensive little pipe tools are referred to as a "smoker's friend." An absorbent paper towel is also handy for wiping off the tobacco juice from the tenon. A soft cloth, such as chamois, flannel or even a clean piece of a discarded T-shirt is useful for polishing the stem and bowl just before the pipe is ready to be put away in the rack. This cloth may also be used to buff the polish on silver or metal fittings that are found on some pipes. Two commercial products that I find ideal for polishing precious metal mountings are Blitz Jewelry Care Cloth for routine buffing, and Flitz, a paste for heavily tarnished metals. Companies such as Comoy's and Alfred Dunhill also market specially treated briar and stem polishing cloths. So much for the basic tools; now, on to the task of actually cleaning the freshly-smoked briar.

After the pipe has cooled and the bowl has been emptied, gently remove the stem from the bowl by holding the bowl in your left hand and carefully twisting the stem and mouthpiece with your right hand. Obviously, left-handed smokers should reverse this procedure. The reason for a twisting rather than a pulling motion is to avoid placing undue strain on the relatively delicate shank, which can easily become cracked even on the best of pipes. Some brands, such as Brebbia, have strengthened the tenons of their bits to make removing the mouthpiece potentially less disastrous, but it still pays to be cautious. Of course, if you have a pipe with a metal screw-in bit, your method of stem separation will already have been pre-ordained.

If you have a pipe in which the stem has become stuck to the point where you fear you might break it if you try removing it by force, here is a final resort: place the pipe in a plastic bag to protect it and put the pipe in the freezer for about a half hour. Sometimes the extreme cold will cause the stem to contract, and it can then be carefully twisted out. Before placing the stem back in the pipe, you might try coating the tenon with graphite from a soft No. 2 lead pencil to prevent it from sticking again.

With your pipe now separated into the bowl and stem sections, take your pipe cleaners and pass them through the airholes of each. It normally takes about three to five pipe cleaners to remove all the stains from the airhole. Next, take a paper towel or soft cloth and vigorously polish the vulcanite or acrylic, paying special attention to the area around the tenon where most of the tars accumulate. If the stem is starting to discolor, give it a buffing with a pipe polishing cloth or a rag coated with tripoli or jeweler's rouge.

The bowl demands a little more attention, for this is where all the combustion has occurred, and will usually require from five to seven cleaners, including one that has been doubled over to serve as a swab for wiping out the tobacco chamber. Pipes using the Peterson system, in which a "tobacco-juice reservoir" has been drilled beneath the bowl, should have this extra accumulation sopped up with an absorbent paper towel and then cleaned with a folded-over pipe cleaner. Be careful when twisting out the bits from such

The benefits of a clean pipe: Before cleaning. This badly neglected briar has a cake that is getting dangerously thick, the top of the bowl has been charred by improper lighting, and the bit is badly oxidized.

After cleaning. First the interior of the pipe was cleansed with grain alcohol, and the bowl was reamed. Then the bit was polished with fine grain wet sandpaper and buffed. After that, the entire pipe was buffed, given a light coating of carnauba wax, and buffed again. A clean pipe not only looks better, it smokes better.

pipes, as the liquid from these reservoirs can spill out, imparting an acrid odor and stain to everything it touches.

When you have finished cleaning your briar (i.e., all the pipe cleaners come out the same color as they went in), you may want to pass a cleaner lightly moistened with a commercial pipe cleaning solvent (available in tobacco shops and referred to as "pipe sweeteners") through the pipe, although I find this usually imparts a slight artificial flavor to the next few puffs I will take on the pipe, interfering with the natural taste of the tobacco. I much prefer using pure grain alcohol, such as the Everclear brand. It used to be available as 190 proof, but it seems some people were using this powerhouse spirit for purposes other than pipe cleaning (image that!), such as spiking the church picnic punch. So now it is only distilled at 153 proof, which is still more than potent enough to dissolve any residual tars, as well as the lining of your stomach. By comparison, most bourbons and scotch whiskies are bottled around 80 to 90 proof. In fact, some adventurous souls even use a pipe cleaner soaked in brandy or rum as a freshening agent, pushing the alcohol-laced wire fluff through the stem and into the bowl. While I have tried this and admit it is great fun on occasions, especially when sucking on the pipe cleaners to remove all excess liquid before passing them into the pipe, it is an abominable waste of a good beverage when commercial pipe cleaning liquids and more properly, grain alcohol, will do the job much better and for less money. No matter which of these alcohol-based solvents you use, do not let them drip onto the bowl of your pipe as they will dissolve the finish.

After my pipes have been thoroughly cleaned and dried, I leave the bowls separated from the stem and allow them to air out for a day or two. The final procedure is to reassemble the pipe (being careful to put the bits back on their correct bowls, always an interesting challenge when one is cleaning a great number of pipes at the same time). Your pipes are now clean and ready to be placed back into their racks, ready for another smoke. Prior to doing so, some pipesmokers have traditionally inserted a pipe cleaner into the pipe in the belief that this helps draw out any moisture that may still be lurking in the briar. But the fact is, if you have thoroughly cleaned and dried out your pipe, there shouldn't be any moisture left. The pipe should be clean and dry.

Nonetheless, for years pipesmokers have been admonished by "experts" to leave a pipe cleaner in the stem of the pipe after thoroughly cleaning it. I myself have fallen victim to this hoax until one day I accidentally discovered THE TRUTH. It was during the construction of a larger den onto my house. Because the older, smaller den was where I conducted my pipesmoking activities, and with the arrival of the contractors and their sledgehammers, my older, smaller den had ceased to exist while we all decided just how many walls the new den was to have. In between arguments, I packed up the majority of my cherished briars and stored them in the garage, saving just enough pipes to get me through the construction period. A short lifetime later, when the job was completed and we at last discovered why the toilets flushed every time the living room lights were turned on, I brought the rest of my briars out of storage. Some had been dutifully put away with the traditional pipe cleaner thrust into their shanks, while others were hurriedly cleaned and packed without the traditional pipe cleaner. I soon discovered that there was absolutely no difference in the smoking quality of my briars to differentiate which ones had been stored with pipe cleaners and which ones had not. In fact, some of the briars which had not been stored with pipe cleaners actually smoked drier than before! I reasoned this was because air had been allowed to circulate through the pipe stem, uninhibited by a thick pipe cleaner. Moreover, when removing those cleaners left in my pipes, they all came out clean, with no faint stains from having soaked up any residual moisture, leading me to conclude that a properly cleaned pipe will remain that way and a dry pipe cleaner left in the stem and bowl will only impede the drying-out process. So save your pipe cleaners for cleaning, not storage.

However, if your briar pipes have been neglected for a long period of time, or if the bit tastes bitter and has oxidized to a grayish white, normal pipe cleaning procedures may not be sufficient and you may have to take your briars to an experienced tobacconist to have them rejuvenated. He will boil out the shank with alcohol, ream the cake to a proper size, clean and polish the bit (even bending or straightening it to a new shape in hot sand if you wish) and polish the bowl with carnauba wax. The exterior of a well cared-for older pipe can usually be brought back to life by carefully cleaning the delicate bit with #400 wet sandpaper, polishing the bit and stem with special pipe cleaning compounds or cloths sold by tobacconists, and then buffing the entire pipe with carnauba wax and a soft chamois or flannel cloth.

The technique for smoking and cleaning a meerschaum pipe is much the same as for briar, with a few notable exceptions:

1. The bare hands should never be allowed to come in direct contact with the bowl, as oils and acids from your skin can affect the wax in the meerschaum and cause the bowl to color unevenly, leaving blemishes over an otherwise smooth area. Some say it is permissible to handle a cold meerschaum pipe, but I never overindulge in this practice out of respect for the fine coloring potential of the material. When smoking a meerschaum, hold the pipe by its stem, or wear a special cloth glove, sold by various suppliers. There are those who scoff at this practice, but a simple glance at their mottled and sparsely-colored pipes tells the entire story. For this reason, some 19th century meerschaums came with special leather cases to protect the pipe bowl from the smoker's hands as it was puffed.

2. Even after a meerschaum pipe has cooled, it is best not to risk blemishing the bowl with residue from your hands that may linger and show up during the next smoke. Thus, when holding the bowl for cleaning, always use a cloth or wear a glove.

3. Be sure to gently scrape away any semblance of cake that starts to form inside the meerschaum bowl. Because of their porous nature, meerschaums need no breaking in and a cake will only act as a barrier that will slow down the natural coloring process of the pipe.

4. Most meerschaums have stems that screw into the shank and may require some force to turn the threads. Be very careful when handling and cleaning these pipes, as they are more fragile than briar.

5. Do not use liquid pipe sweetener on meerschaum pipes, as it will soak into the bowl. Years ago, castor bean oil was used for cleaning meerschaums, but thankfully those days are over. Instead, use plenty of pipe cleaners, including the wire bristle "Reem 'n Clean" type. Due to their absorbency, meerschaum pipes can be smoked day after day without tasting sour, as long as they are thoroughly cleaned between smokes.

6. To help your meerschaum age and turn color quicker, try blowing a little smoke on it as you puff. The micro-

scopic particles of smoke will be absorbed into the surface, while they also work their way to the outside of the bowl from the burning tobacco. My wife calls this "cheating," but with all the pipes I've got, I may not be around long enough to see my meerschaums turn a rich, chocolate brown. Why not help nature a little? Years ago, some meerschaum pipes were artificially aged by coating them with a mixture of dyes and linseed oil and then applying heat to the pipe. However, I prefer the natural smoking method, as it gives these pipes a deep mellow color that has yet to be artificially duplicated.

No longer as popular as it once was, the smoking of clay pipes is still worthy of mention. Although I find it historically and meditatively interesting to smoke a clay pipe on certain occasions, they are somewhat impractical in that they must always be held in the hand. To try and clench one in your

Two innovative methods for carrying tobacco: (L) The Davidoff pouch features a gold spring hinge that pops the pouch open for easy filling; (R) the Comoy's pouch fits flat in your pocket, but can be spread open like a box for easy access to the tobacco within. The silver and ebony tamper was made by Otto Pollner of Bünde, Germany.

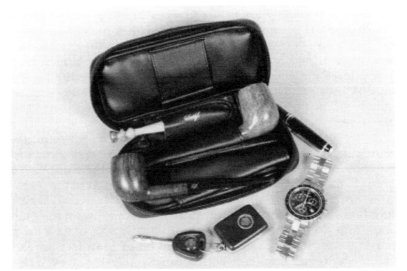

A pipe pouch, like this two-briar model from Davidoff, can hold all of the necessities for a civilized outing, with plenty of room for a spare pipe, tamper, tobacco, and even business cards.

For longer journeys here and abroad, Michael Butera's elegant silver and leather traveling case is ideal. There's plenty of room for a tamper, tobacco pouch and miscellaneous accoutrements, plus the protective leather divider folds over to reveal storage for four pipes. Shown with a Butera leather tobacco pouch are two frequent flier straight grains: (top) a Stokkebye "B" grade and (bottom) an Alfred Dunhill five star Rhodesian. A Charatan Supreme from the 1950s peeps out from the leather divider.

teeth will invariably break the pipe, either in your mouth or on the floor. However, clays will season after only a few bowlfuls and soon become surprisingly mellow. In time the bowls will turn off-white and eventually a yellowish brown and sometimes may even go to "black and oily," like the famed clay of Sherlock Holmes, although it will take many years of steady smoking and a lot depends on the composition of the clay itself.

By virtue of its fragility, the clay pipe is a low-maintenance means of enjoying pipe tobacco. The stems are too narrow and fragile to permit the use of all but the thinnest of pipe cleaners, and reaming the bowl is totally out of the question, unless you enjoy breaking pottery. Instead, when finished smoking a clay simply fluff out the ashes, let the pipe cool, and then carefully wipe the inside of the bowl with a paper towel. If the pipe becomes caked or starts to smoke "sour" (a common malady with aromatic tobaccos), even the rankest clay can be thoroughly cleaned by simply placing the pipe in a blazing fireplace. After the ashes have cooled, remove the pipe and it will be as white as the day you bought it. I discovered this little secret quite by accident, when my favored "Christmas pipe," a white clay churchwarden that had become nice and blackened with age, suffered a terrible fall one day. Being clay, it did the only thing expected of it and broke. Dismayed at losing such a faithful companion that had spent so many late nights with me reflecting upon the eventual fate of the world, I tossed it into the fireplace. The next morning while cleaning out the ashes, I made the discovery I now share with you. The clay bowl was as white and clean as snow. But to prove Cicero was right and that there really is nothing new under the sun, years later I read about this very same cleaning process for clays in a book entitled, *Tobacco: Its History and Associations*, which was written in 1859.

What's that you say, you have a dirty clay but don't have a fireplace? No problem; a butane lighter will work almost as well. Simply hold the pipe upside down and waltz the butane flame inside the bowl. Be sure to hold the pipe by its stem, as the bowl will get very hot. Place the lighter as far inside the bowl as possible without extinguishing the flame. You'll immediately see a bluish glow as the heat vaporizes the foul smelling particles. Repeat this process two or three times, let the pipe cool, and then gently wipe the inside and outside free of soot with a paper towel. A sniff of the newly sterilized bowl will tell you that you have done your job well.

Mastro de Paja's swing-out pipe rack looks like a square block of wood until it is "unfolded" to hold three pipes. Shown are (L) a Larsen straight grain Pearl with ivory and brown cumberland bit; (R) Brebbia's designer series, this one by Pierre Müller of Geneva; and (rear) a Julius Vesz B grade bent featuring a gold banded owl with diamond eyes.

This Davidoff pipe rack is made of Macassar wood. The silver cradles are large enough to easily hold an Alfred Dunhill ODA and an extra large Ferndown silver mounted Bark bulldog.

I would assume there'd be no reason to point this out, but just in case: only preform this technique with a *clay* pipe. The flame will scorch a briar pipe and will very likely set a corncob on fire.

With your pipes cleaned and polished, the final step is to store them in a rack. In America, the practice is to place the bowl lower than the stem, the theory being that any remaining moisture will drain away from the mouthpiece and settle in the thicker portion of the pipe cleaner in the heel. The European technique has been just the opposite, with the bowls up and the stems pointing downward. This was often the fashion in the 19th century (many Victorian- era pipe stands reflect this practice). The objective was that all of the remaining juices would flow away from the bowl so as not to taint the next smoke. Of course, this would have put those acids right at the tip of the mouthpiece, but I guess nobody ever thought of that.

In reality, both of these practices originated during a time when there were no pipe cleaners as we know them

The handmade glass and gold pipe rack by Wilhelm Eser of Ars Vitri in Germany is an excellent way to display your prized briars. Each rack is signed and dated by the artist. The pipes are (L to R) a Comoy's Collector; a 1971 Alfred Dunhill Shell with bamboo shank, and a perfectly grained six-sided panel by Erik Nørding.

today. Back in the early years of pipesmoking, chicken feathers were used instead, a less than effective method to be sure. As a result, many pipes were put away "wet" by necessity. But as we have seen, today's pipes can be cleaned and dried to perfection, without a trace of moisture. Thus, whether stored with the bowls up or down no longer makes any difference. The main criteria is to store your pipes in a rack or ventilated case where fresh air can circulate, not locked up in sealed container. For this purpose, many of the current pipe stands and ventilated display cases are the best means for storing pipes. Just be sure you buy a rack that holds more pipes than you own. That way, you'll always have an excuse to buy more.

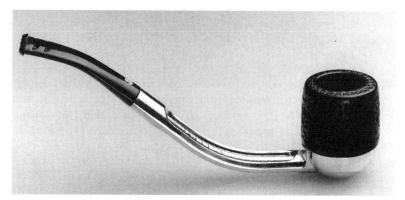

Although it originated in the United States, the British-made Falcon pipe, with its metal body and multiple interchangeable bowl system, has achieved worldwide popularity.

This naturally finished Larsen straight grain is one of the best values in a high-grade pipe. It uses plateau briar normally reserved for handmade pipes, but this paticular version is machine made.

Chapter 4

PIPE TOBACCO —
A NEVER-ENDING
QUEST

As anyone who has ever tamped a pipe is well aware, there is more to puffing on a briar than merely grabbing the first colorful tin of tobacco you see. Even when sufficiently versed in the nuances of pipesmoking, properly packing a carefully chosen briar with the wrong tobacco can completely negate your pipesmoking experience. Pipe tobacco is like a cologne that may smell good in the bottle but it can take on a completely different characteristic once it is on the skin, depending on the body chemistry of the person using it. And so it is with tobacco. Each smoker has a different chemical balance within his body that determines what tastes good and what is distasteful.

There are three sensory criteria for selecting a pipe tobacco: taste, strength, and aroma. All are variables, because each smoker may perceive the same tobacco differently. In addition, a tobacco's taste and strength may change, depending on whether it is smoked inside or out-of-doors, as well as how long it has been stored and where it has been kept. The type of pipe can also affect the taste of a tobacco. Some woods, such as the sweetness of a cherrywood pipe, have a more pronounced influence over certain tobaccos. In addition, the briar of a pipe can sometimes be tasted within the flavor of the tobacco, but thankfully, this is not the norm. More often, the wood is subservient to the tobacco, which is as it should be, for there are far too many variables in blended tobaccos to be compatible with the various geographical sources of briar being used by today's pipemakers. On the other hand, meerschaum pipes tend to retain the flavor of the previous bowlful, while clays are the most neutral tasting pipes of all, which is why I use them for tobacco testing.

Aroma is the third variable in a pipe tobacco. It is the most noticeable to those around you, but what smells pleasant to one individual may not necessarily smell good to another. Personal choices are also influenced by the environment in which a pipe is smoked, with one type of tobacco being more suitable early in the day, another selected for after the evening meal, and perhaps a third being chosen because it is more acceptable to family members and co-workers. Thus, choosing a tobacco is as individualistic as choosing a pipe, for no single tobacco can ever be "perfect" for everyone.

However, to give us some background information to aid in making a decision, it may help to know a little bit about the plant itself, where it comes from, and how it gets from the ground and into our pipes.

To begin with, there are about fifty different varieties of tobacco, the most common of which is *Nicotiana*, originating in the Western Hemisphere, although the plant is now grown worldwide. Besides the United States, tobacco flourishes in Canada, Brazil, Africa, Italy, Greece, France, Germany, Sweden, New Zealand, Yugoslavia, Hungary, China, Russia, Japan and Puerto Rico. After all, it is a weed, although rarely

When the raw, dried tobacco leaves are first brought into the blending factory, they are inspected and smelled for aroma, for the nose is one of the best indicators of quality. Here Hans Petersen of A&C Petersen of Denmark checks a hogshead container of newly-arrived Virginia leaf.

has a weed been cultivated with such reverence. Tobacco is also grown in India, but frankly, the quality is not always the best. There is, however, an excellent sweet and spicy pipe tobacco exported from Cuba; it is most notably available in Dunhill's Havana blend and can be purchased in bulk from their Jermyn Street store in London. Unfortunately, thanks to the embargo, it may not legally be brought into the United States.

Only three of the *Nicotiana* varieties have any real interest for the pipesmoker. The most popular, of course, is the historic *Nicotiana Tabacum*, a native of South and Central America and the very plant that our hero John Rolfe shanghaied from Trinidad to Virginia in 1612. Second in popularity, especially for those smokers preferring English blends, is *Nicotiana Rustica*, a native of Mexico which is now grown in Europe, Africa and Asia and which is responsible for producing the rich-tasting Turkish, Latakia and Sumatra tobaccos that we often enjoy late at night accompanied by a glass of single malt. Last in the tobacco trilogy is *Nicotiana Persica*, the smallest member of the tobacco family and named because it was originally grown only in Persia. In the United States, where much of the world's pipe tobacco used to be grown, the top producing states are North Carolina, Virginia, Kentucky, South Carolina, Georgia and Tennessee.

The eyes and hands are also used to inspect raw tobacco for strength, color, vein structure, and overall texture.

I have always found it somewhat ironic that in order for North American pipesmokers to obtain some of the highest quality European blends, the tobacco must first be grown in the United States, shipped overseas for processing and packaging, and then exported back to America.

Four hundred years ago pipesmokers had to be content with what they could readily obtain in the way of pipe tobacco. There was not much selection available. In some of the more primitive areas, dried tobacco leaves or cornsilk was the optimum choice. However, today we have a decided advantage over our ancestors, as a casual glance in even the most moderately stocked tobacco shop will reveal numerous tins and pouches from a multitude of suppliers, each containing a different mixture, not to mention the tobacconist's own lineup of private house blends. To give you an example, in Great Britain there are currently 350 different pipe blends, but in Germany, there are over 700! The U.S. lies somewhere in between, although in reality, cyber-shopping has made the made the choices endless. And therein lies the problem. Where does one start?

To begin with, it helps to know a little about the primary tobaccos that are used for blending. Throughout my pipesmoking career, I never found a single source that described what each of these tobaccos were, so that I might better understand what a specific mixture contained in terms of taste and personality. I finally ended up compiling a list of my own, which I now share with you.

Burley — A rather coarse, sun-cured leaf that was first grown in America in 1864. Today Burley primarily comes from Tennessee, Kentucky and Ohio, although it is also grown in Brazil, Italy, Africa, and Japan. The leaves are a light yellowish green to yellow-brown in color. It is an extremely mild tasting tobacco. In fact, Burley has an almost transparent flavor when used by itself, and this characteristic, combined with its unique ability to absorb the flavorings that are added to aromatic tobaccos, makes Burley an excellent host and binding agent for these popular mixtures. Consequently, Burley is one of our largest tobacco crops today.

Cavendish — A generic term for tobacco that has been flavored with sugar, maple or rum and then heated and pressed in recurring cycles to give it a darker color. This process produces a thick, sweet and comparatively mild taste when added to other tobaccos.

Latakia — A very expensive and distinctively Oriental tobacco that was discovered quite by accident in the early 1860s. Latakia takes its name from the village of Lattaquié in northern Syria. During one of the harvests, a number of tobacco leaves were hung in the rafters of a native hut to air dry. The leaves were subsequently forgotten. Over time, smoke rising from the cooking fires permeated the leaves. Eventually, someone noticed the tobacco in the rafters, took it down and remarked on the heady, smokey flavor. Out of curiosity, the natives and leaf buyers tried this tobacco in their pipes and a new chapter in blending was born, much to the delight of English tobacco fanciers everywhere. Today Latakia is not only grown in Syria, but Cyprus and Lebanon as well. It is sun-cured and then dried over open fires, a time-consuming and exacting process that makes it a very expensive tobacco. Latakia is dark brown to almost black in color and is one of the few tobacco plants in which the stem and leaf ribs (being the sweetest-tasting portions of the weed) are used, along with the leaves themselves. Latakia produces a rich, heavy smokey taste, and is usually found in most quality English mixtures. When blending Latakia, a little can go a long ways, but for the connoisseur, too little is never enough.

Maryland — Unlike Virginia, most of Maryland tobacco is grown in the state for which it is named. It is a rich brown in color and is often used to increase the burning characteristics of other tobaccos, such as Burley.

Perique — A very rare, slow burning, and strong-tasting tobacco with an air of mystery about it, due to the fact that Perique is only grown in a small, 500-acre triangular section of land in St. James Parish known as Grande Pointe, in the bayou country of Louisiana in the extreme southern part of the United States. Because its growing area is so close to the Mississippi River, the mineral-rich soil helps give Perique its legendary pungency. Attempts to grow it elsewhere have failed. Although Perique has been around since the early 1800s, today there is only one producer left. The cultivated tobacco is soaked in plum juice and fruit pulp, then twisted into tight bunches called "torquettes" and placed in wooden barrels, where it is put under tremendous pressure via an iron press. The leaves ferment in their own juices, then they are aired out, moistened with water, and placed back under pressure in the barrels. This process is repeated for as many as six times, and even continues while the leaf is warehoused.

Each year there is less Perique produced as farmers abandon the area for more economical crops. As a result, many blenders have stopped using it. The rarest of all tobaccos, it is blackish brown in color with a uniquely rich flavor and aroma. Perique is one tobacco that should never be smoked by itself; smoking straight Perique is the equivalent of having a lobotomy. However, when used by skilled blenders, Perique can produce an even-burning, distinctive-tasting mixture that couldn't exist without this mysterious tobacco.

Turkish — Not a single strain, but rather a broad classification of at least a dozen rich, sweet and oily tobaccos that are actually grown in Greece. It is a quality leaf that burns well and evenly and has a wide range of slightly aromatic tastes. Turkish tobacco is rarely used in pipe tobaccos, although it is found in some of the more exotic blends.

Virginia — Its name is somewhat of a misnomer, for although it was first grown by English colonists in Jamestown, today it is far more prominent in the tobacco fields of North and South Carolina, as well as Florida and Georgia. It is even grown in Japan. Virginia tobacco is most commonly a bright yellow color and for that reason is called "bright" tobacco by growers, although a dark Virginia does exist. This tobacco is also found in cigarettes, but it is only the more costly higher quality and thicker leaves that are used for pipe tobacco. Dark Virginia is most commonly found in mixtures and is more aromatic than the light. However, bright Virginia, when smoked, has a pleasantly sweet, woodsy taste, which makes it popular in many blended pipe tobaccos, although too much Virginia in any mixture will tend to burn "hot." Used in moderation, however, it lends a superb flavor to practically any blend.

Normally all pipe blends start out with either Burley, Cavendish or Maryland tobacco as a base, then other tobaccos and flavors are added. Virginia, Latakia, Perique and Turkish tobaccos tend to make heavier blends. Burley and Cavendish mixtures create a light taste. Certain countries, such as England, Denmark, Holland and Germany, typically produce tobaccos which are uniquely characteristic of a "national taste" that serves as an undercurrent to the blend itself.

True to the very nature of the flavor it will ultimately produce, the very best tobacco is grown in the very best of soils. The southern states of North America have some of the most fertile soils and climatically ideal environments for growing the tobacco plant; the average yield is over 1,100 pounds of tobacco per acre. Furthermore, a single plant can produce a quarter pound of tobacco, and if you want another useless fact, approximately four pounds of processed tobacco will produce one pound of ash.

Although tobacco is now being grown worldwide due to the higher costs of American-grown leaf, in the northern hemisphere the pipe tobacco saga begins when the delicate seedlings are planted in canvas covered trays in March. They are kept indoors to slowly germinate, thus getting a head start on growth until the weather warms up. Then from May to June (it usually takes from 6 to 10 weeks for the young plants to become strong enough), the tiny plants are transferred to the great outdoors and planted in fields. Once strictly a hand operation, this is now largely done by machine, wherein each seedling is pressed into freshly prepared earth at precisely 40 centimeters apart. Each row is one meter from the next, in order to give the tobacco room to grow. It is a very exacting science. Depending on the country and climate, the growing season can last from three to five months. During that time, the tobacco plants are subject to disease, mold, and insect infestations and must be watched over and nurtured like a delicate child.

Scientific fertilization and in some cases, crop rotation, is needed to produce a healthy harvest. The plants are carefully pampered like the valuable commodity that they are. Prior to harvesting, each plant is 'topped," whereby the uppermost stems and the top flower are cut off so that more of the plant's strength goes into the leaves. The "suckers," or new shoots that spring out of the stems as a result of the topping process, are also trimmed away so that none of the growing strength is deprived from the main body of the tobacco leaves. The tobacco plant is very sensitive to both moisture and heat, conditions which can cause discoloration and even holes in the leaf. As the healthy leaves ripen, they begin turning yellowish green in color, sometimes with yellow spots, and they become rougher and thicker in texture.

Finally, the plants are ready for harvesting. This takes place as early in autumn as possible, as the tobacco leaves are highly susceptible to frost. However, with the world's climate starting to change, we are now seeing later harvests, and sometimes a second planting is possible, thereby increasing the total tobacco crop for a given country and year.

During the harvest, the leaves to be used for pipe tobacco are trimmed from the center and top portions of the stalk (the bottom leaves are traditionally used for cigarette tobacco). Only full, mature leaves are cut or "primed," leaving the plant to nurture the remaining leaves. In this way, a single plant will eventually produce a greater yield of tobacco.

The old methods of hand weighing and stripping the tobacco leaves with sharp knives, whereby the stalk is removed from the leaves and a worker "feels" whether or not the tobacco is dry enough, have largely been replaced with modern machinery and in more sophisticated operations, with complete automation. However, many growers still feel that hand picking is a more exacting technique, as workers can physically sort over the immature green leaves and only remove the mature growth. If immature "green" leaves are harvested, they will never properly age, no matter how well they are cured and blended later on.

Just as the curing (drying) process of briar is crucial to the final smoking qualities of the pipe, so is the curing (fermentation) process critical to the ultimate flavor of the tobacco. Curing dries the tobacco leaf, which starts out with a moisture content of around 75% to 85% and is eventually evaporated down to 25% or less This is achieved by one of three methods:

1. **Sun-cured** (also called air-cured) — This was the original curing process for tobaccos. It is a natural, open-air method of drying, wherein the tobacco leaves are hung from poles and allowed to air dry in the sun and warm breezes, using no artificial heat. Sun-drying is still commonly used for dark tobaccos, primarily Orientals from Greece, Turkey, Southern Italy, Albania, Russia, and Syria.

2. **Flue-cured** — First begun in the 19th century. As in sun-curing, the tobacco leaves are suspended on poles, but the drying process is accelerated and controlled by filling the sheds, via metal flues or conducting pipes, with hot air heated from 90 to 170 degrees Fahrenheit. Notice that the delicate leaves are not subjected to any smoke. Flue-curing greatly speeds up the sugar-conversion process of the leaves and gives them a color that ranges from yellow to reddish brown. When you read about "flue-cured Virginia tobacco," this is what they are talking about. Normally, only air-curing and flue-curing are used for most pipe tobaccos.

112

3. **Fire-cured** — Instead of sunlight, steam or hot air, an actual smoldering oak and sawdust fire is used in the drying sheds to create a hot, smoke-filled environment that eventually dries out the tobacco leaves. The entire process takes about 40 days. The result, as you might expect, is a very smokey-tasting tobacco.

After the curing process, the tobacco leaves are graded according to color and texture. Then they are aged (also referred to as fermenting), whereupon the leaves are stacked and stored for anywhere from six months to three years, depending upon the tobacco and the blend it is to be used for. This fermenting cycle is a very crucial process, for it will help determine the final flavor, color, and aroma the tobacco will have.

The numerous varieties of aged and cured tobaccos are then sold at auctions, which are normally held from the end of January until the beginning of April. The bidders for the various pipe blend manufacturers carefully inspect each basket or bale of tobacco before making an offer. The selection of your favorite pipe tobacco is therefore a very personal business, even before you put your match to the bowl, for someone else has already decided how that particular mixture is going to taste; it is up to you to determine whether or not their decision was the right one for you.

The tobaccos are then shipped to blending companies, primarily in the United States, Great Britain, Germany, Holland, and Denmark. Here, they are steamed and brought back to life with moisture. In blending a tobacco according to specific recipes, various tobaccos are used from different harvests, so that even if a particular tobacco is in short supply due to a poor growing season, the blender can incorporate other tobaccos from different vintages to maintain a taste and aroma that smokers of that particular blend have come to expect. Thus, it is like creating a cognac, in which various distillations from different vintages are used to maintain a consistent taste, aroma, and color. This objective has become more challenging in recent years as the growing areas for tobacco have changed, as the varying mineral contents of different soils in different countries produce different flavored leaf. That is why a can of Rattray's #7 Reserve today, which is blended in Germany, does not taste exactly like the blend did twenty years ago when it was made for the family by Mick McConnell in England. And nowadays, most people don't realize that even Mick's blend differed ever so slightly from the original family's, as some of his tobacco was coming from a different source. But compare a currently-made can of Rattray's #7 Reserve today with one packaged three years ago, and I defy anyone to taste the difference, for once these recipes are in place with a particular blender, there is a strict, almost fanatical adherence to consistency.

After a brief storage period, the tobacco is put through machines that clean the leaves and remove the woody stems, although a few manufacturers still prefer to have this operation done by hand. For some tobaccos, such as Latakia, the stem, or portions of it, actually comprise an important part of the final flavor, and therefore are not discarded.

Next comes the blending process, one of the most critical operations for any pipe tobacco. It is much like preparing a gourmet meal; it is the various ingredients, their proportions and even how they are served (packaged) that creates the ultimate flavor and personality of the tobacco, which directly translates into the enjoyment a pipesmoker will receive from it. Because each tobacco has its own burning rate, color, flavor and other characteristics, which also includes the way it is cut, the object is (or should be) to produce a blend in which each of these elements complement the other. It is not surprising, then, to learn that each pipe tobacco company has its own individual formula and methods of blending their various tobaccos. These blending recipes are among the most jealously guarded secrets in the industry, for they hold the key to a popular tobacco's success. Obviously, each one is unique.

Nevertheless, all blends can be divided into two categories: English and Aromatic. English blends have been with us the longest, as up until 1986, tobacco additives were not allowed in Great Britain. English blends are pure, unadulterated combinations of specific types of tobacco, usually Latakia and other Oriental varieties, each imparting its own distinctive taste to the final product. Many purists prefer English blends because they get the true taste of the tobacco leaf. English tobaccos often taste and smell stronger than aromatic blends but as a rule, they generally smoke drier. They are the favorite choice of many pipesmoking connoisseurs as well as those people who like to drink their whiskey straight.

Aromatics, on the other hand, are usually blended with a Burley or Cavendish base and are often milder than English tobaccos. In addition, they have had a flavoring agent added to provide an enhanced taste and an extremely fragrant aroma, something which often endears aromatic smokers to everyone around them.

At this point, if the tobacco is to be an aromatic or semi-aromatic blend, casings are added. "Casing" is simply another word for flavorings, and they are responsible for the person sitting next to you saying, "My, your pipe tobacco smells just like chocolate!" These tobaccos are sprayed with diethylene glycol or propylene glycol, a food grade additive that helps keep the tobacco moist. Then, mixtures of sugar, glucose, molasses and actual food flavorings are added to the aromatics, according to the recipe. Specific flavorings used include cocoa, treacle, plus essences distilled from licorice and vanilla. Nuts and fruits, especially kiwis and litchi nuts, are also found in some blends. But there's more. In addition to chocolate, honey, rum, cherry, apple, peach, banana, coffee, and even bourbon, malt whisky and rum, a host of other tasty treats can be added to the aromatic leaves at this point in their manufacture. In fact, were it not for the noticeable lack of baked potato and steak flavorings, one could make a complete meal out of tobacco casings alone.

There are also some casings that are added specifically for the *aroma* of a pipe tobacco, much to the delight of non-smokers when you light up. This is a top flavoring that is misted onto the finished blend just before it is packaged. The flavors of this top flavoring are more subtle than the casing itself, but they are extremely important, as they must harmonize with the main flavors.

Whether English or aromatic, once the tobaccos are blended they are aged, so that the various leaves — which sometimes can be as many as 40 different varieties — will "marry" and mellow out their flavors. Then the blend is packaged and shipped to your local tobacco store, where you eventually arrive with empty pipe and pouch in hand, glance over the multi-hued array of packets, tins, and glass jars and scratch your head, wondering if you should open your wallet just to find out what a certain brand tastes like.

Choosing a tobacco, especially for the newer pipesmoker who is unfamiliar with many of the brands, is much like ordering a meal in a restaurant that has a 24-page menu. The selections are so vast and most of it sounds so good, but if we have never eaten there before, or cannot trust the waiter to make a suggestion, our freedom of choice turns into frustration. And for the first-time pipesmoker, the menu might just as well be written in a foreign language.

Unfortunately, this situation is compounded by many of the tobacco manufacturers themselves, or more properly, their marketing policies, for few actually tell you what that particular blend smokes like, even though they know this

Some of the more popular soft-pouched pipe tobaccos include these aromatic Cavendish, Virginia and Burley blends from around the world.

information. But if one were to believe in the promotional copy in magazines, brochures, and on tins, then virtually every tobacco in the world "smokes sweet and cool, slow-burning and mild." By virtue of using the same adjectives for different blends, we are erroneously led to believe that everything smokes the same and that we are going to love it. A detailed description would be an improvement. From a packaging standpoint, a color photo of the blend could be printed on the label, or better yet, a plastic window could be cut into the tin so that we could actually see what is inside the package without opening it. After all, in addition to its taste, the visual appeal of a blend is carefully calculated by the blenders. Shouldn't we be allowed to have this knowledge before making a purchase?

It would also be helpful if all the tobacco companies got together and devised some form of industry grading system for each of their blends, which would then be printed on the containers. All we want are the aged and blended facts. For instance: Tobacco Taste: strong, medium, mild. Aroma: sweet, smokey, floral. Burning Rate: slow, medium, fast. In previous editions of my pipe books, I proposed a numerical rating system so that the strength of all tobaccos could become public knowledge. Since then, I have devised the HPH Strength Factor in my cigar books. It has worked out quite satisfactorily and I see no reason why we can't adopt it for pipe tobaccos as well.

Basically HPH stands for Highly Prejudiced Hackerscale and the numbers range from 1 (extra mild) to 3 (brutally strong), with most of the more popular tobaccos falling into the HPH 2 category, which is medium-mild. In between these three classifications we have the half-measures of 1.5 and 2.5. It is called the Highly Prejudiced Hackerscale because it is mine, I am highly prejudiced when it comes to tobacco, and it is based upon my perception of a particular blend's strength, rather than flavor. It is not a "better than" grading; the numbers simply are a way to gauge the strength of a tobacco. We will actually get more into the HPH scale in the next chapter, when it is applied to over 100 different blends.

But strength is not the total tobacco story, for there is also taste, and like various foods at different mealtimes, the taste of a particular blend may fluctuate and change as it is smoked during different times of the day. I have always felt that it was impractical to expect a pipesmoker to be inseparably wedded to the same tobacco day after day, week after week. Variety is what keeps the taste buds tingling and it is the thrill of popping off the lids of new tins every now and then that keeps the spirit of adventure alive and fresh around our pipe racks.

Admittedly, there is a sense of security in finding one stable, likable pipe mixture and sticking with it throughout the years, like a favorite flannel shirt. Every pipesmoker should have a few of these blends to fall back on when no more surprises can be tolerated at the end of the day. Having such treasures is indeed one of the pinnacles of a pipesmoker's life. A Victorian writer named A. M. Jenkinson certainly felt this way in 1897, in his classic volume of tobacciana entitled, *Whifflets*,

" . . . there is nothing among men that will quicker bring even a righteous man into scorn and contempt than the use of a poor mixture by which he spoils other people's pleasure and degrades his own palate . . . Indeed, appreciation of good tobacco is a test of true gentlemanly instincts. . . a man who smokes bad tobacco when good tobacco is abundant. . .has his sense of taste and smell deficient or blunted. . . it follows that if his judgment on tobacco be wrong, it is very likely to go astray on other important things."

But just as we smoke a different pipe to match our different moods, why not vary our tobaccos, in an effort to better satisfy our fluctuating cravings and to match our pipesmoking to the biorhythms of life? For example, a very mild HPH 1.5 tobacco might be ideally suited for the "morning pipe," while an HPH 2 mixture of medium strength would go well in the mid-afternoon, as an aid to settling lunch and calming one's outlook on the rest of the day. In the evening, a slightly headier HPH 2.5 brew would help us relax as only a well-packed briar can do.

Of course, these are only generalities and many a pipesmoker may prefer to stick with his HPH 1.5 "morning pipe" all day long, or perhaps limit his smoking to a single Latakia-laced HPH 3 bowlful of the evening blend, no matter what time of the day it is smoked. Personally, I enjoy medium English tobacco in the evening and have a hard time adjusting to the heavy, thick clouds of Latakia and Perique early in the day. On the other hand, I drink red wine with fish, like very spicy foods, and have been known to eat onion sandwiches late in the afternoon. It is all a matter of personal taste, which is why I hesitate to recommend movies, music, or pipe tobaccos.

Of course, if one has plenty of money and lots of time, it would be one of life's great adventures to obtain a packet or pouch or tin of every tobacco available and smoke a bowlful of each to determine whether or not you're going to like it, taking copious notes, throwing the foulest- tasting of the batch at the dog and keeping the pleasanter blends with you until at last, by process of elimination, one would have discovered *the* ultimate tobacco for his or her own personal taste. But life is not that simple and it takes a lot of time to smoke a lot of tobacco, although now that I think about it, that's exactly what I've done in Chapter 5.

One of the variables you will be faced with is whether to try an English or aromatic blend. Both types of tobaccos are popular. Up until a few years ago, aromatics were the reigning choice by a three-to-one margin in countries like the United States and Germany. However, with the recent influx of cigar smokers now turning to the pipe, in America at least, the ratio is evenly divided between English tobaccos and aromatics, as cigar smokers are used to the slightly more pungent taste of pure tobacco. As to strength, both English and aromatic tobaccos can run the gamut of being mild or strong, ranging from HPH 1.5 to 2.5. You really have to smoke both in order to make a decision.

However, aromatics frequently have an annoying habit of smoking "wet." That is, as the heat from the pipe permeates the tobacco, some of the aromatic additives condense into liquid, which ends up coagulating in the heel of the bowl along with the natural moisture from the burning tobacco. Often this situation is compounded with saliva from the smoker's mouth. Thus, we end up with an annoying "gurgle" with every puff, which is a signal to start searching for the pipe cleaners. Not all aromatics are guilty of this phenomena, but a great many of them are, and it is up to the smoker to chose between a rich and sometimes stronger but drier smoke, or a sweeter, milder one that will require the use of more pipe cleaners. However, there are even some English blends that smoke wet. One solution is to smoke these tobaccos in a pipe with an absorbent filter or in a clay or meerschaum, both of which are more absorbent than briar. But do not smoke an unusually wet tobacco in the porous corncob, which would simply be asking that historic pipe to commit suicide by drowning.

Another factor to consider in selecting a blend is how the tobacco has been cut, which determines the physical shape of the leaves you will be putting in your pipe bowl. The type of cut can affect the burning rate and therefore, the taste. A coarsely cut tobacco will burn slow and is a good choice for the fast and heavy puffer as well as for the smoker looking for a milder taste (blend notwithstanding). A finely cut tobacco or one composed of thin strands of leaf will burn faster and somewhat hotter, although this is ideal for the slow, meticulous smoker, as he does not have to puff as much in order to keep his pipe lit.

The basic cuts are shag, cube (occasionally called "chop" cut) and ribbon (sometimes referred to as "long cut"). English blends traditionally are made up of long ribbon cuts because they use Virginia as a base, and Virginia is a long cut tobacco. These finer, string-like strips are easy to keep lit. Burley is almost always a cube cut, which is slow burning because of its thickness. In Victorian times, shag was a very coarse-cut tobacco and was the favored smoke of Sherlock Holmes. Today, however, shag has come to mean exactly the opposite, as it is now a finely cut tobacco which is often found in Cavendish blends.

Another form of tobacco still occasionally encountered is Plug or Cake tobacco, which is also called Navy Cut. Plug tobacco has been soaked in honey, which acts as both a bonding agent and a sweetener. The blend is then molded by

The three basic cuts of pipe tobacco are (L. To R.): Ribbon, usually found in most English blends; Cube, often encountered in aromatic Burley blends, and Flake, which must be rubbed out in the hands in order to smoke it.

120

packing or forcing the gooey tobacco into holes (or "plugs") that traditionally were drilled into hickory logs. The tobacco is then placed under 12,000 pounds of pressure for 8 hours or more. Popular in many rural areas in the 19th century, plug tobacco could be conveniently carried in pocket or pouch. When ready to smoke or chew, a measured amount would be cut off with a pocket knife or perhaps a Green River or a Bowie, depending on the geographic area of the smoker. Storekeepers used heavy iron "plug cutters" to chop off a plug, which was sold by the slice. It was then broken up into smaller pieces or rubbed out by hand for pipesmoking.

Because it is an older form of tobacco usage, perhaps we should say a few words about how to prepare caked tobacco for our pipe, as very few of us have our great-grandads around to ask. First, place a small-sized portion of the tobacco in the palm of your hand. Then rub this tobacco between your palms, gently breaking it up. You can further refine the process by breaking up the strands into smaller pieces with your fingers. By tearing the tobacco into thick or thin strips, you can actually control the burning rate. The correct preparation of cake tobacco is as important as properly packing it in your pipe, otherwise it will not be an enjoyable smoke. The object is to eventually get it to a physical state where it can

Flake tobacco comes in many tastes and shapes. In the lower right corner next to the Escudo "rounds" is a modern-day escudo coin from Portugal.

be trickled into your pipe bowl and properly tamped. Improper rubbing will leave clumps, which will impede the airflow, making your pipe not only hard to light but even harder to keep lit. Now you know why they came up with "ready rubbed" blends!

Obviously, part of the reason cake tobacco is not as popular as it once was is due to the added effort it takes to prepare it for smoking. But breaking up cake or plug tobacco and "rubbing it out" between the palms of the hands is actually a very relaxing activity, especially if you are sitting by yourself on the back porch on a crisp autumn day. However, it's not the sort of thing you'd want to do at a formal dinner party or on a first date.

Flake tobacco is similar to caked blends, as it has been pressed under heat to create a compact cake, but is then sliced into small, thin "boards" before it is put into a tin. Like plug tobacco, the smoker has to roll the flake in his hands to break it up prior to filling his pipe. A "ready rubbed" tobacco is simply flake tobacco that has been rolled in huge metal drums prior to packaging, breaking up the flakes into smaller pieces for easer packing. "Rounds" are blends that have been rolled into a thick rope and then sliced, of which Escudo is the best example. It, too, should be rubbed out, although some smokers simply shove rounds and flakes into their pipes and light them as they lay. I have tried this but find that the tobacco does not stay lit as well.

No matter what the cut of your tobacco, or whether you favor aromatic or English, the trick in finding the perfect blend or blends is to experiment and discover new brands, new tins, and new mixtures. For me, the adventure of searching for the "perfect" tobacco has never ceased. Consequently, much to the chagrin of the tobacco blenders, for many pipesmokers, myself included, there is no such thing as brand loyalty. We are always ready to try something new, even though we usually go back to our favorites. However, given the law of averages, it is not surprising that we find many tobaccos are very close in taste, while others are so unique as to be totally unduplicated. A good case in point are the soft pouched tobaccos of Clan (one of the most popular aromatics in the world), Captain Black (an aromatic Burley and black Cavendish blend), and Kentucky Bird (a wonderfully mild Virginia actually blended with real rose petals). There are smokers who will smoke only these blends and nothing else (somewhat of a problem for those Americans who smoke Clan, as it is no longer being imported into the United States). On the other hand, truly dedicated followers of the rich English tobaccos can often make a painless switch between Dunhill's Royal Yacht, London Blend by Timm, and Rattray's Red Rapparee.

I know of one friend who always carries four or five packages of Condor with him whenever he takes an extended trip, for fear of running out. This, of course, borders on paranoia, as Condor is an extremely popular tobacco, especially in England, where my friend lives. However, now that it is no longer imported into America, it makes sense for him to bring his favorite tobacco with him when visiting the States, just as many Americans are now bringing pouches of Clan back with them from Europe. To be sure, when traveling to Europe I often take my own tobacco, but it's not because I am afraid of finding nothing to smoke. It's just that, ironically, European tobaccos (which I smoke almost exclusively) are usually cheaper in America due to our slightly lower taxes,

Tinned and boxed tobaccos can hold many pleasant discoveries. The author found his first tin of Baker's Street in a German railway station. "My Own English" is a private mixture purchased in Stuttgart while visiting the Mercedes factory. Indian Summer was found in Frankfurt, looks American, but is actually blended in Ireland. The Planta Pipe Pointe tin has an indented lid that can be used as a pipe rest and the Japanese tobacco comes with a matching box of matches.

although this situation is changing, due to a vocal and selfish minority of anti-smokers.

But I still end up buying brands in Europe that I cannot get in the U.S., not only to smoke, but also to acquire the tins, which I collect. After all, today we have some of the most picturesque assortment of tobacco packaging in the history of pipesmoking, with multi-colored tins such as Indian Summer, W.Ø. Larsen's Classic, and the nostalgic Nightcap and Early Morning Pipe from Dunhill all being prime exam-

Collectable tobacco is the newest trend among pipesmokers. The Balkan Sobranie is from the late 1970s, the Craven Mixture, McConnell Scottish Blend, and Robert Lewis tobaccos are all from the 1980s and the Orient Express Special Mixture No. 15 is from the 1950s. All are sealed, except for the Orient Express, which the author was smoking at the time he took this photo.

ples. It is hardly surprising that after the tobacco has been smoked, these empty tins are often saved.

But now a new trend has started, for today not only are the tins collected and traded, but also the tobaccos themselves. This has led to groups who, for example, began hoarding tins of Rattray's while it was still being made in England — before the blending operations were moved to Germany. When some collectors discovered that Escudo was being discontinued, they started buying up all the tins they could find. Interestingly, now that Escudo has been brought back, these people are smoking the new blend but still saving the old, which is priced on the collector's market at a higher cost than a current tin of Escudo. And when it was announced in 1998 that St. Bruno, Three Nuns, Clan, and Condor were no longer going to be imported into America because of all the anti-tobacco litigation, U.S. smokers started bringing these brands back from Europe, both to save or trade for a tobacco they didn't have, and, of course, to smoke. It seems we always want what we can't have. Consequently, there is an active collector's market for rare, old, and unopened tins of pipe tobacco.

As an example, I was recently offered three times what I paid for an unopened tin of British-blended McConnell's Scottish Mixture. And at a pipe show some years back, I remember a GBD pipe collector who started foaming at the mouth when he saw me pop the lid off a new tin of long-discontinued GBD tobacco and start filling my pipe with it!

Additionally, there are serious pipesmokers who save and age their tinned tobaccos, much as one would store and age cigars or wines. In many cases, this does enhance and mellow the flavors over a brief span of years, but it should be remembered that when you buy your tobacco, it has already been aged by the manufacturer. There is rarely any need to age it further, although Virginia-based blends can keep a long time but the pungent Oriental tobaccos will peak after 8-10 years. Do we really want to wait that long for a good smoke? Well, some people do.

Not surprisingly, there are special limited edition tobaccos being made just for collectors, although not as many as you might think. The yearly Christmas offerings of Gold Block and the past Limited Edition Premier Grand Cru tobaccos by Alfred & Christian Petersen are just two examples. More recently, on September 24, 1998, when Alfred Dunhill had a special pipe night at their London store, they reintroduced a limited number of tins that duplicated the private blends of notable past customers, such as novelists P.G. Wodehouse and Rudyard Kipling. Now, those were blends to collect, but as you might have guessed, I smoked all of mine.

There is no easy "first-time" solution to finding the right tobaccos for your taste. One method is to tell your tobacconist what you want, try his recommendation and then proceed from there to either stronger or lighter, more aromatic or more English-style blends. In this manner, sometimes the tobacconist with a large assortment of house (private) blends can save the smoker a lot of time and trouble, as he is able to mix a number of different tobaccos together for you to create a blend that is all your own.

Creating a private tobacco blend can be one of the most rewarding aspects of the pipesmoking hobby, whether your tobacconist does it for you or you do it yourself. It is relatively easy to purchase a small selection of various tobaccos from your local pipe shop for further experimentation at home. Just try to stay with the same type of cuts (cube, ribbon, etc.) as it will make it easier to control the burning rate of your finished blend. Imagine adding a bit of Latakia to a Cavendish, for example. Or perhaps putting a pinch of the forbidden Havana leaf in with an English mixture.

In addition to many cigar smokers now taking up the pipe, we are also getting converts from the nicotine-laden ranks of heavy cigarette smokers. Consequently, although a light to medium strength (HPH 1.5 — 2) tobacco is normally my recommendation for the first-time pipesmoker, the new owner of a briar who is used to going through multiple packs of cigarettes per day may find more satisfaction from some of the heavier HPH 2.5 blends (see Chapter 5). The hardest thing cigarette smokers have to learn, however, is *not to inhale*, so that they still get the feeling of a nicotine "hit," but are no longer drawing the smoke into their lungs. Interestingly, from a health point of view, most of the tobaccos used for pipesmoking only contain about three percent nicotine, and of course, none of it is inhaled.

A commonly asked question among new pipesmokers is, "How much tobacco should I buy?" That, of course, depends on how much tobacco you smoke and whether you are satisfied with your present mixture. In the 1700s, it was common for the average man to smoke two pounds of tobacco a year. Of course, pipe bowls were smaller then, roughly one-half to two-thirds the size of a medium-sized briar today.

Nowadays, tobacconists normally consider a pound to be a one month's supply for the medium to heavy pipesmoker. However, I often smoke only one or two bowlfuls a day, increasing my tobacco usage in the autumn and winter months and unconsciously cutting back during the spring and summer. Consequently, I find that a pound usually lasts me for a good four to six months. But then, I often experiment with new brands and in addition to my main supply, there are always four or five opened tins scattered about the den or hidden under the living room chair, where the cat has been playing with them. Therefore, the answer to the question of how much tobacco to buy is simply that the heavier smoker should buy in a larger quantity while the lighter or occasional pipesmoker might be satisfied in purchasing smaller packets; normally, handblended tobacco is sold by the pound and it is not unheard of to ask for a half-ounce of tobacco just to try it. The pre-packaged tins and foil-sealed containers of tobacco usually come in 1-1/2 ounce (42.5 gram) packaging, a not altogether unwieldy amount.

However, no matter how much tobacco you buy, in order to be smokable, it must be kept properly humidified. Ideally, this means it should be kept at a constant temperature of 70 degrees Fahrenheit and at a humidity level of 70 percent. Now, unless you live in a self-enclosed, scientifically controlled glass bubble, it is realistically impossible to maintain that degree of perfection. In fact, the only place I have ever seen it done is in the storage warehouses of the major tobacco companies. Many modern smokeshops pride themselves on their walk- in humidors, which create a semi-controlled atmosphere for their bulk tobaccos, which are kept fresh until placed on the counter in smaller glass humidors. However, in our homes and offices, it is a slightly different story. Normally, the inside temperature is kept around 68 degrees F, but sometimes in the winter, the heat is turned up and that can quickly dry out our tobacco. Here is where humidity, which is a little more controllable, comes into play.

If not kept properly humidified, loose tobacco will quickly dry out, no matter what the temperature. Of course, individual packages of pipe tobacco are sold in pressure-sealed tins (which make a reassuring "whoosh" when opened for the first time, telling you that the tobacco was packed fresh and still is) or in air-tight foil pouches. These can keep tobacco fresh for months — sometimes even years. Normally, aromatics, because of the moisturizers in the casings, will stay fresher longer than English blends. However, I recently opened a tin of Dunhill 965 that I have had for over ten years and it still was fresh (I wasn't aging it; I just forgot where I had put it). But once the air-tight seal is broken, your tobacco will quickly dry out if not kept moist. The best way to do this is to use one of those small individual moisturizers sold by tobacconists. I keep one in my pouch and another in my humidor, just to play it safe.

Speaking of humidors, or tobacco jars as they are called in Europe, they are one of the most important accessories a pipesmoker can have. A humidor is simply an air-tight container with a refillable moisturizer used for storing your tobacco. Humidors are normally made of materials that will not affect the taste of tobacco, such as porcelain or wood. Stay away from plastic containers, as they can impart an odor to the tobacco. The moisturizing device can be anything from a piece of organic sponge affixed to the lid to porous clay "buttons" made especially for this purpose. The Credo moisturizers that were originally developed for cigar humidors work especially well. No matter what type of unit you end up with, only use distilled water in your moisturizer, to guard against the formation of mold. The wetness of the humidor's

Pipe Able's limited edition Sherlock Holmes humidor (see Chapter 6) is flanked by a Peterson Lestrade from their Return of Sherlock Holmes series and a calabash by Andreas Bauer.

moisturizer should be checked once a week, especially if the container is constantly being opened and closed numerous times each day, or is in a particularly warm or dry environment. Not only is a humidor indispensable for keeping your tobacco fresh, it can also be used for breathing new life into a dried-out blend and making it smokable again. But be careful not to get your tobacco too wet, or it will be hard to keep lit and will smoke bitter and moist. Overly humidified tobacco can create mold, which means the tobacco must be discarded.

While on the subject of mold, an age-old method for keeping pipe tobacco moist has been the ruin of many a pouchful of weed and should be publicly dispelled once and for all: it is the practice of placing a slice of apple or pear or other moisture-bearing fruit in with your favorite blend. Not only will this interfere with the natural taste of the pipe tobacco, but the fruit will immediately start its natural "rotting process" which, if left in the pouch or humidor long enough, will cover your tobacco with a nice fluffy white mold, thereby ruining your ration of *Nicotiana Tabacum* beyond resurrection. The slightest trace of mold will also render your pouch or humidor completely useless unless it can be sterilized by cleaning it thoroughly and then setting it out in the sunlight. This was one of the many self-taught lessons I learned in college, when I first started smoking a pipe. Not being able to afford a proper humidor, I kept my meager supply of Old Hayseed in a plastic jar with a screw-top lid. Noticing that it would quickly dry out, I asked a few "knowledgeable" pipesmokers what to do and promptly got the standard instructions about the apple slice.

It just took one week for mold to form, emanating from the moist apple and spreading over my entire month's supply of tobacco. I reluctantly tossed the musty tobacco out, washed the plastic jar, and refilled it with another dollar's worth of blend. But those little spores were still at work, alive and kicking but invisible to the naked eye. This time it took them three weeks to finally surprise me with a whole new family of white fuzz. I was tempted to keep the mold for a pet (I couldn't afford a dog in those early years), but finally chucked the whole mess out in the trash and made do with weekly purchases of various sundry tobaccos that came in sealable pouches. The moral of this story is: keep all moist organic material away from your tobacco.

Another questionable means of not only keeping your tobacco moist but also of flavoring it, is a "secret" usually passed on to an unsuspecting nimrod by an old smoker, who advocates sprinkling a few drops of rum or brandy onto your tobacco. Frankly, I view this practice as either a poor waste of good liquor, or a good waste of poor liquor. In either case, it is not necessary, as there are aromatic tobaccos today that have been professionally cased with everything from malt whisky to bourbon and in varying degrees of strength to meet any taste requirement. So keep your rum and brandy in their respective snifters, not in your humidor. (Still, I know you're going to try it once; everybody does. Just don't make it an ongoing practice.)

For the first time pipesmoker as well as the curious expert, there is a great deal of smoking enlightenment to be had by buying one of the variety packs of tobacco put out by various tobacco firms, or by having a tobacconist make one up for you from a selection of his house blends. In this way, for very little expenditure, you can experiment with a broad range of different tobaccos, just as you would at a wine tasting party.

The more you smoke your pipe, the more you realize that tobacco is a paradoxical substance, for it can act as both a stimulant and a relaxant, depending upon the mind-set of the smoker. Some people in competitive industries such as publishing, finance and entertainment use the pipe as a method for sharpening their wits, while after hours these same individuals use the combination of pipe and tobacco as a means for "coming down" after an adrenaline accelerated day, preferring to smoke their pipe in the solace of the evening, when the phones are silent and never-ending deadlines can be temporarily forgotten.

Pipesmoking is a pastime that is best done in moderation. Consequently, whether the tobacco is strong, medium or mild does not really seem to matter in the ultimate analysis of things, for it is simply a matter of how the tobacco treats us, rather than how we treat it. Yet throughout our pipesmoking experience, whether it lasts for only a few years or until the Final Puff, there will always be the real or the subliminal quest for perfection, the chance of finding Utopia in a foil-lined packaged or sealed tin, much the way J. M. Barrie did when he wrote his classic volume of *My Lady Nicotine*, in which he extolled the virtues of his favorite mixture, the Arcadia:

". . . I seldom recommend the Arcadia to men whom I do not know intimately, lest in the after-years I should find them unworthy of it. But just as Aladdin doubtless rubbed his lamp at times for show, there were occasions when I was ostentatiously liberal. If, after trying Arcadia, the lucky smoker to whom I presented it did not start or seize my hand, or otherwise show that something exquisite had come into his life, I at once forgot his name and his existence."

For the true pipe connoisseur, tobacco is a precious commodity. No one knows this better than those pipesmokers who suffered through the war-ravaged shortages of World War II, when many individuals had to grow their own tobacco if they wanted to smoke at all. I will never forget visiting a small but well-stocked tobacco shop in The Hague on a trip to Holland a few years ago. The proprietor, a man many years my senior, recognized me from both the German and American editions of my pipe books and greeted me like an old friend. It turned out we were also both members of the Confrérie des Maîtres-Pipiers de Saint-Claude.

"I have something for you." he said, putting a kindly hand on my arm. And with that he went into the back of his store and brought out a small, fragile paper package, tied with string and brown with age. "Here," he said, gently placing the package in my hand. "It is the last bit of pipe tobacco that I grew during the war. I've saved it all these years. Now I want you to have it, so that you will never forget how precious things are."

Indeed, tobacco represents a way of life and a means of enjoyment that is unique in the world, and only known to those of us who smoke a pipe. And that is the real secret of picking the right blend.

Irish Whiskey, whether in the bottle, on the label, or in the tobacco, provides a flavorful bond between snifter and pipe.

Elegant spirits, like these premium cognacs, are perfect after-hours companions for some of the more heavily structured pipe tobaccos.

132

Chapter 5

TOBACCO TASTER'S MENU OF BLENDS

No matter how attractive the ad, how enticing the package, or how pleasant the aroma, you can't tell what a tobacco tastes like until you smoke it. And until you do, the next best thing is to have someone tell you something about how it smokes. That is why I have written this chapter. Although it cannot possibly cover every tobacco in the world, think of it as a primer, to help get you started.

The problem for most pipesmokers trying to explore new frontiers of tobacco tasting is the cost of each tin or pouch. That can make it a very expensive adventure, from which you may never return. After all, if you don't like the blend, you're still stuck with it after the first pipebowl. Over the course of time, you'll be paying quite a substantial sum of money just to discover which blends are your favorites and which are not. Of course, this discovery is part of the fun of pipesmoking, but one should have a guide so that you will not wander off on paths that you may not want to take. Therefore, in an effort to lead you through the maze of pipe blends staring out at you from catalogs and facing you on your tobacconist's shelves (in addition to saving you enough money on unwanted blends so that you can easily recoup the cost of this book), I have decided to include this long-needed chapter on tobacco tasting.

I must admit that in my smoking past, I have been reluctant to stray too far from my own designated preferences. These include, as far as tobacco is concerned, lots of Latakia, a touch of Perique (more so on some days than others), and other Turkish and Orientals according to my mood. But I realize there are tastes out there other than mine, which is obviously why we have literally hundreds of different blends. To be sure, not only is there a perfect tobacco for everyone, there are *many* perfect tobaccos for everyone. But by no means can we hope to smoke them all, although that is a noble goal for one's lifetime.

However, to give the reader a head start in choosing a number of blends with which to experiment, I am listing over one hundred tobaccos that I have studied, smoked, and recorded in tasting notes. Some of these tobaccos are familiar friends to my pipes and me, for we have been smoking them for years. Others are newcomers, both figuratively and literally. Also, given the fact that the internet has now made tobacco buying an international activity, I thought it might be interesting to include tobaccos from various countries that may not be readily encountered. And in addition to most of the major brands, I have included representative samplings of tobaccos made by some of the smaller American blenders, such as McClelland, Cornell & Diehl, and Esoterica Tobacciana, which is actually made in Britain for an American importer. Many of these blends are enjoying immense popularity among pipesmokers in the U.S. and elsewhere. The growing selection of tobaccos worldwide bodes well for the pipesmoker of today, for the more choices we have, the better our chance of finding those "perfect" blends.

At the Royal Theodorus Niemeyer factory in Holland, a master blender carefully checks the various leaves that are used to give flavor to the company's many blends.

134

Through the course of my smoking research, I have made some very positive new discoveries. Yet ironically, although never before have we had so numerous choices, it seems that

At a tobacco testing lab, the author inspects some of the many different tobaccos that will eventually be used to make up a specific blend.

nowadays we have less time in which to smoke these various blends in order to make a decision. And while it is fine to experiment with new tobaccos, sometimes we just want to sit back and enjoy the smoke, with no surprises. That was one of the overriding reasons that inspired me to write this chapter.

Admitting my penchant for English tobaccos, I have, in the interest of fairness, included aromatics in these tastings. Which brings up a point about taste.

By no means do I decry Cavendish or cased tobaccos. They are all worthy of my pipes at certain times. Why else would I smoke McClelland's Christmas Blend on December 24th? Or try Larsen's Choice in my Larsen pipe and a bowl of Castello Optimo in my Castello Fiamatta just for the experience of doing it? Besides, taste is subjective, so who am I to tell what you will like or dislike? That is a personal decision that only you and your taste buds can make.

Strength, on the other hand, is a bit more subjective. It is far easier for me to tell you that a certain tobacco is mild, or even spicy, as opposed to good or bad. Therefore, I have adopted the same criteria for tasting pipe tobacco that I have successfully used in describing cigars in *The Ultimate Cigar Book*. That is the much heralded HPH strength rating. HPH stands for Highly Prejudiced Hackerscale and the numbers range from 1 (so mild you will have to see if there is any smoke coming from your pipe to tell if the tobacco is lit) to 2 (medium strength and the range most of the more popular blends will fall into), to 3, a blend so strong it can change a curved pipe into a straight and make a Canadian out of a Lovat. Very few tobaccos reach an HPH 3 and when they do, you will probably need a note from your doctor to buy a tin. In between these ranges we have the half-stops of HPH 1.5 and HPH 2.5 for those tobaccos that are medium light or slightly stronger than medium strength. It must be emphasized that these HPH ratings are not a numerical scorecard telling you which tobacco is better than another. The HPH scale is strictly a gauge in which to measure *strength*.

But don't forget the "Prejudiced" part of the HPH nomenclature, for this is my scale according to my likes or dislikes of the tobaccos I am testing. Therefore, my personal tastes will naturally influence my perception of a blend. For example, when it comes to wines, I favor heavy Cabernet Sauvignons. I like thick medium rare steaks and prefer the smokiest malt whiskies from Islay. Someone else, on the other hand, may be partial to white wines, vegetable salads, and the delicate floral character of lowland single malts. Therefore, what is an HPH 2 to me might very well be a 2.5 or even a 3 to someone else. So you have to take the taster's palate into account. But considering the lack of any other industry standards, the HPH scale works very well. Who knows, in time we may start to see it used on tins and in reviews as the one universal method by which we can at least get a running start on deciding whether or not a specific tobacco is for us.

As far as rating tobaccos on a numerical scale of good-better-best, as in wine, I find that method to be totally inappropriate for pipesmoking. There are simply too many variables in each blend, such as the cut, the numerous tobaccos that make up the blend, the burning rate and the overall flavor. For example, how would you rate a peach flavored aromatic over one with whiskey casings? Or an English blend that used no Latakia? Is a ribbon cut really better than a pressed flake? And what about the burning rate? No, pipe tobacco is much too individualistic, as are pipesmokers themselves, to be subjected to a predetermined scale of what they should or shouldn't like.

I should say a few words about the methods used in creating this tobacco tasting menu. For personal reasons, I was not about to smoke any of the aromatics in my favorite briars, as casings tend to permeate the wood and forever taint it with essences of fruits, berries, and chocolate coffee. Nothing wrong with that if you ordinarily smoke aromatic tobaccos. In fact, melding your pipe to the blend is part of the fun. But most of my pipes have been broken in with a preponderance of Latakia and Perique (although I do keep a few "aromatic briars" in the rack just for scientific purposes, so I confess to not being totally prejudiced). But briar pipes — especially their cakes — tend to absorb the taste of the blends that are smoked in them and that lingering flavor would undoubtedly affect the pure taste of the next test tobacco to come after it. Even in a new pipe, as we learned in Chapter 1, the type of briar and the way it has been cured can affect a tobacco's taste. So wooden pipes were out. Likewise, meerschaum pipes, because of their great porosity and the wax used to treat them, also eliminated themselves for any serious tobacco tasting, unless, of course, I wanted to use a new meerschaum for each new bowlful. This had a great attraction for me, as I saw it as a possible way to quickly acquire more than a hundred new pipes as I tested more than a hundred new tobaccos But even though I have an extremely understanding wife, she has somehow caught on to these little schemes and is no longer so easily fooled. So in the name of matrimonial harmony, meerschaum was eliminated as a tasting vehicle.

Corncobs were a consideration. They are inexpensive, but also suffer from excessive porosity, which would make one tobacco taste a little like the one smoked before it. No, when everything else was considered, I arrived at the conclusion that only a clay pipe would do. It met all of the requirements: First and most importantly, clays impart little outside influence to tobaccos, so the purity of the blend being tested was assured. Secondly, clay pipes are relatively inexpensive, so even if one became tainted with an overly strong English or soaked with heavily cased blends, it could be replaced

Tinned tobaccos hold a special fascination for both the smoker and the collector. Some of the more interesting designs available today are shown surrounding a 19th century smoker's plate, indicative of the close relationship between tobacco and food.

without much of a financial strain. In addition, most authentic clay pipes, using 18th and 19th century molds, have fairly small bowls, so if I did not care for a particular tobacco, I wouldn't have to smoke too much of it. Of course, if it turned out to be a favorite, the tin or pouch was humidified and saved for a later date, when I could smoke it at leisure without needing pen and paper and total concentration.

Tobacco testing is not something that can be done rapidly. You can't test smoke more than three or four different tobaccos in a given day. Otherwise your sensory capacities can become overloaded and your palate loses its ability to separate and analyze flavors. This is especially true when smoking particularly strong or distinctive blends. We've all have the experience of being able to taste a tobacco long after the bowl has been emptied. In the wine industry they refer to this as a "long finish." But when tasting tobaccos, it is best to pace oneself, even if you are used to smoking multiple pipes a day. Tobacco tasting is different than tobacco smoking, just as wine tasting is different from wine drinking. Also, in some cases, I separated my tasting sessions with a quick repast of bread and mineral water between bowls, just to clear my palate.

The end result of all this is the chapter you now have before you. Some tobaccos are described in more detail than others, depending on the information I was able to obtain and frankly, my mood while smoking that particular blend. Nevertheless, I hope my experiences and personal notes will help you discover some enjoyable blends and that this sampling of tobaccos will serve as an inspiration that will lead you to other blends, so that you may derive greater pleasure in your pipesmoking.

ALSBO BLACK — A mild black Cavendish and Virginia blend cased with vanilla. Sweet and medium in strength. HPH 2

ALSBO GOLD — African and Brazilian golden Virginia leaf, light Burley, and black Cavendish are blended and cased with a combined essence of dried fruit with a preponderance of apples. There is also a nut-like walnut and flowery flavor that lurks within the blend. HPH 1.5—2

ALSBO SILVER — Don't let the name or the package color fool you — it's really black in color, thanks to a Cavendish base with dark Virginia that has been cased with vanilla and Oriental flavorings. Very sweet smoking yet light. An HPH 2, which proves that silver is heavier than gold.

AMPHORA BROWN — Not as sweet tasting as the red, but still noticeably aromatic. HPH 2

AMPHORA GREEN — This is the mildest of the Amphora mixtures, nice and light, with just a touch of sweet fruit flavor and hazelnuts. HPH 1.5 —2. It is extremely popular in Europe but as of 1999, it was no longer imported into America, where it was also highly regarded.

AMPHORA RED — A full flavored aromatic, packed with Burley, Kentucky, Oriental and Virginia tobaccos and producing a rich fruity aroma. This was a favorite of the late actor, William Conrad. HPH 2—2.5

ASHTON OLD CHURCH — A mellow aromatic. HPH 2

ASUKA SMOKING MIXTURE — This is blended in Japan by Japan Tobacco Inc., but it tastes so classically English, you expect to see the words "London" on the tin. It is wonderfully dry smoking with a rugged, medium smokey flavor. HPH 2—2.5

BALKAN SASIENI — The Danish version of Balkan Sobranie is being made by Peter Stokkebye and comes in at HPH 2—2.5. It looks, feels, and smells like the original blend, just as smoky, maybe a little bit subdued. The Danish influence, I suppose — not necessarily a bad thing. However, it is slightly lighter in taste than the original British blend (which I remember well). Nonetheless, this early 20th-century mixture of Virginia and Latakia tobaccoes brings back fond memories.

BALKAN SASIENI LIGHT — Introduced in the fall of 2000, this Danish blend has throttled way down on the Latakia and pumped up the Virginia to create a much milder HPH 2 interpretation of an old English favorite.

BALKAN SOBRANIE — Another one of the world's great English tobaccos, formerly of Sobranie of London at the historic address of 34 Burlington Arcade (don't look for it now, however; it is gone) and which is now being made in Germany for the European market. It is a wonderfully rich and full-bodied blend of light and dark Virginia with Macedonian leaf and a healthy measure of the finest, smokiest Latakia. For years I have used this tobacco as a measure against all other English blends. In the United States, due to copyright complications, it is now sold under the name of Balkan Sasieni, and is being made in Denmark. Consequently, it is a slightly different blend from the European version. A definite HPH 2.5 that is best reserved for the evening hours.

BENTLEY — Sold by the makers of the German-based Bentley Pipe Company, this is an extremely mild blend of Burley, Virginia and Maryland tobaccos. With so many naturally subtle leaves, its HPH 1.5 strength is hardly surprising.

BILL BAILEY'S BALKAN BLEND — A deep, rich, and heavy smoke, full of Latakia (over 40%!), a touch of Kentucky and — as if you needed it — a pinch of Perique. Do not smoke this on an empty stomach. HPH 2.5

BORKUM RIFF — Blended in Sweden, manufactured in Germany, and cased with American bourbon, this heavily aromatic blend is like smoking the United Nations in a pipe. It is a popular international smoke. HPH 2—2.5

BORKUM RIFF CHERRY CAVENDISH — If you like rich, whipped cream and cherry-filled desserts and enjoy cookies between meals, you're going to love this blend. HPH 2

BORKUM RIFF ULTRA LIGHT — With a hint of vanilla and chocolate, this is an aromatic tobacco that's been toned down, for those who think they may not quite like an aromatic tobacco. HPH 1.5

CAPSTAN — A pleasantly mild blend, made with Virginia tobaccos. HPH 2

CAPTAIN BLACK GOLD — Primarily golden Cavendish, giving this mixture a rich yellow color. Hence its name. It is a highly sweet aromatic laced with vanilla. HPH 1.5—2

CAPTAIN SPICE — This ultra aromatic vanilla-cased Cavendish has been around for as long as I can remember — and that's a long time. One of the Tinder Box chain's most popular house blends, even nonsmoking bystanders love its aroma. The thick black coarse cut leaves are slow-burning and exceedingly flavorful. If you love aromatics, you'll love this. HPH 2—2.5

CASTELLO OPTIMO — An Italian brand made in Denmark by old friends Hans and Jens Petersen. A medium strength blend of black Cavendish, Virginia, and Zimbabwe tobaccos flavored with orange, vanilla and rum to produce a thick and hearty aromatic. The tobacco is cut as thick as the taste. HPH 2—2.5

CELLINI — A very light orange cased aromatic from Berlin. HPH 1.5

CLAN — A medium-strong aromatic consisting of both air-cured and sun-cured tobaccos, primarily Virginia, Indonesian, and Latakia. The flavor is sweet with hints of chocolate and caramel overtones. Because of its extremely pleasant aroma, it is a fairly safe tobacco to smoke around others who don't, assuming they aren't the violent type. There are 3 types of Clan mixtures: the original Clan Aromatic, Light Aromatic, and Mild Cavendish. This brand emits one of the most distinctive and enjoyable aromas of any aromatic pipe tobacco. Unfortunately for U.S. smokers, it has been withdrawn from the American market, so you will now have to buy it in Europe. European pipesmokers, of course can still readily find it and it is one of the most popular pipe tobaccos in Britain. HPH 2

CONDOR READY RUBBED — Thicker cuts of tobacco provide a slow burning English tobacco with a full, semi-rich taste. HPH 2.5

CORNELL & DIEHL #063 (non-tinned) — Not a particularly imaginative name, but a pleasant spicy-sweet and mild English blend just the same. In fact, it's one of the mildest Perique mixtures you'll ever smoke. Light and medium dry in taste. HPH 1.5—2.

CORNELL & DIEHL BAYOU NIGHT (non-tinned) — As the name suggests, this is a blend laced with Perique and aged with stoved red Virginia, Latakia, Turkish and held together with rough cut Burley. Yet for all that, it is a surprising mild HPH 1.5—2. That's what Burley can do for a blend. Spicy and gently sweet, it is in fact one of the mildest Perique mixtures on the market. It also burns nice and dry, making it a pleasure for those who desire the taste of English without the heavy smokiness usually associated with these blends.

CORNELL & DIEHL BRIGADIER — Cornell & Diehl's Brigadier is a mixture of cubed Barley, black Cavendish, Latakia and Perique with a casing of apricot. It is very mild and aromatic, hardly what you would expect from a real brigadier. HPH 2

CORNELL & DIEHL RAJAH'S COURT — This is an American blender's attempt to duplicate the old Alfred Dunhill Durbar blend, but it smokes a bit lighter than the original Durbar, which has been recently brought back by Alfred

Dunhill. Red and bright Virginia, Turkish, and Latakia give it a spicy, medium flavor, with just the slightest hint of sweetness underlying with gentle smokiness. HPH 2.

CORNELL & DIEHL RED STAG — I'd smoke this one just for the name. A combination of both red and flake Virginia, plus Turkish and Latakia. It is slightly perfumed and smokey. HPH 2

CRAVEN — Originally named after Britain's Third Earl of Craven in the 1860s. Actually, it's not quite the same as it once was, for it is now produced in three versions: an Aromatic, a Mild Flake and a Mild Ready-Rubbed. But alas! There is no longer a Craven A, the fabled fictitious "Arcadia blend" of which J.M. Barrie wrote so eloquently about in his classic Victorian treatise, *My Lady Nicotine*. (Ironically, the resultant publicity of having his name on the tin became too much for the Scottish author, and he soon switched to John Cotton's). Still, the current tins contain a pleasant, slightly sweet and medium strength aromatic, staying in the HPH 2 range.

CRAVEN EXTRA — An aromatic offshoot of the current Craven blend, only this newest addition features dark Virginia for a slightly stronger HPH 2—2.5

DANSKE CLUB BLACK LUXURY — The tobacco is as dark as its name. Four different Burleys and six types of Virginia make up this blend, which is aged for a minimum of 2 months. The result is a full, thick vanilla-tasting HPH 2.5 aromatic.

DAVIDOFF COOL MIXTURE — A very slow-burning HPH 1.5—2 tobacco, thanks to thickly cut black Cavendish, roasted Burley and just a bit of Virginia cut plug. Probably one of more elegant "entry-level" blends.

DAVIDOFF DANISH MIXTURE — Virginia, Burley and black Cavendish keep up Denmark's preference for aromatic flavors and mild to medium strength. HPH 2

DAVIDOFF ENGLISH MIXTURE — Medium-cut leaf, easy to pack, blended with Virginia, Burley, Latakia and a hint of Perique. A gentle smoke. HPH 2

DAVIDOFF LIGHT MIXTURE — One of the newer blends, designed to appeal to the smoker who wants a tobacco that is not overbearing. This one certainly isn't, thanks to a mild blend of Virginia, Burley and black Cavendish, which tends to bump up the fruitiness a bit. HPH 1.5—2

DAVIDOFF MILD MIXTURE — As you might have guessed, even though the same basic tobaccos are used as in the Light Mixture, the flavor intensifier has been cranked up slightly, to an HPH 2.

DAVIDOFF ORIENTAL MIXTURE — Turkish and Latakia tobaccos are blended in with Burley and Virginia leaf to produce a semi-strong yet flavorful smoke. HPH 2.5

DAVIDOFF ROYALTY — A medium English style mixture made with mature Virginia and Oriental leaf and an accent of Latakia. HPH 2

DAVIDOFF SCOTTISH MIXTURE — A blending of Virginia, Burley and Kentucky tobaccos plus Oriental leaf starts to bring this mixture into the English taste category, but a light casing of Scotch whisky ends up producing a definite aromatic quality. It has a noticeably pleasing aroma as a benefit for those around you. Try this one with a snifter of single malt Scotch from the lowlands. HPH 2—2.5

DUNHILL EARLY MORNING PIPE — There are some non-smokers who buy this just for the tin. It is pure nostalgia. But thankfully, the tobacco is well worth the experience, mild as it is. A smooth and easy blending of Oriental, bright Virginia, plus Middle Belt red and Virginia leaf produces a slow burning, subtle tasting tobacco that is indeed the perfect, easy-going blend for that "first pipe of the morning," as Nigel Bruce once said to Basil Rathbone in an early Sherlock Holmes movie. HPH 1.5

DUNHILL STANDARD MIXTURE MEDIUM — A tinned English blend that is exactly what its name implies. A medium-strength mixture composed primarily of Virginia, Latakia and Oriental tobaccos that have more character than strength. An effortless way to enter into the world of English tobaccos. HPH 2

DUNHILL AROMATIC — One of the new soft-pouched series, this blend of Virginia tobaccos from the U.S. and Brazil, pressed and rubbed out and cased with fruit, was not possible back in the days when England had laws forbidding flavorings in their commercially blended tobaccos. It has been introduced to appeal to smokers who want a mild, non-obtrusive blend that still delivers flavor. It is very mild, fruity and aromatic, but smokes a bit wet. HPH 1.5—2

DUNHILL ROYAL YACHT — A tobacco steeped in history and reflecting a time when the royals visited the Duke Street store (which is now called the Jermyn Street store, although the only thing to have moved is the front entrance) on a regular basis. Not as strong as it looks, this is an elegant, medium-strength smoke with a hint of sweetness. HPH 2—2.5

DUNHILL MY MIXTURE 965 — One of my all-time favorites and definitely a tobacco that I wouldn't mind being marooned with in a Rocky Mountain cabin or a remote island resort. Three different blends are used to make up this medium-strong and wonderfully palate-filling English tobacco. The complexity of taste is a result of flue-cured leaf being mixed with aromatic Burley, along with smokey Latakia and Turkish leaf which have been steam-heated. The result is a classic blend with essences of stately manor halls, campfires and a faint touch of floral sweetness to round it all out. As an added benefit, it is one of the few tobaccos that burns exceedingly dry with a wonderful grey-white ash. HPH 2—2.5

DUTCH BLEND — Very aromatic and mild. A popular pouched tobacco that was introduced in the late 1980s to appeal to the newer smoker. HPH 1.5

EDWARD G. ROBINSON — An old American brand that was introduced in 1946 and named after one of the most famous American motion picture "tough guys," who had his picture on the package. It was owned by Robinson in partnership with noted Hollywood film director George Sydney (*Harvey Girls*, *Pal Joey*, *Showboat*, *Viva Las Vegas*, etc.). Although Edward G. Robinson usually portrayed gangsters and was often filmed smoking a cigar, in real life he was an avid art collector and an enthusiastic pipesmoker. This mild aromatic is still being produced, although very few people know of it anymore. HPH 2

ERINMORE — Originally blended by Murray Sons & Company back in the 1920s, it has changed little since then. It is one of the most popular tobaccos coming out of Ireland. The blend contains orange and mahogany flue-cured tobaccos that perfectly intermingle with Burley, stem-pressed Cavendish and a touch of Virginia to produce a medium aromatic with a pleasant and flowery flavor. The aroma is wonderfully mild and fresh, like the subtle fragrance of wet herbs in the garden after a Spring rain. Upon lighting, there is a taste of honey and new mown grass with a definite hint of oak from the wood aging. A perfect tobacco for afternoon or early evening. HPH 2. The Erinmore Flake is a slightly stronger HPH 2—2.5 in strength and aroma.

ESCUDO NAVY DE LUXE — A classic older English tobacco of a type that was popular in the 1800s and was first commercially produced by the old British tobacco firm of Cope's. In the 20th century it was a favorite of Alfred Sasieni when his factory was making the early One-Dot pipes for Europe and the Four Dots for America. The name Escudo comes from the Portuguese word meaning a gold coin (as an aside, the escudo is still a coined form of currency in Portugal, although it is no longer made of gold), because in the early days of sailing vessels, the crew would take some of the tobacco leaves that were carried in large barrels called hogsheads, and roll them up tightly in sailcloth, which was then tied with twine. In a few weeks, after the aged and dried tobacco rolls had married their favors, they would be unwrapped and cut into slices for breaking up and smoking in clay pipes of the period. Because these tightly compressed rolls of tobacco were about the diameter of a Portuguese gold coin when thinly sliced...well, you know the rest. The Cope brothers were traders and knew of these "escudos" being smoked by sailors on their ships. They thought it was a novel idea and about 1870 they began making a commercial Escudo brand. Once vacuum tins became perfected, the Escudo blend spread all over the world. Because its manufacture was so labor intensive, Escudo was more expensive to make than most blends, and consequently was always considered a high class tobacco. Its high cost eventually caused it to be discontinued in 1994, but due to demand from loyal customers, it was brought back in the fall of 1998 by the Japan Tobacco Company. It is now made in Denmark by Hans & Jens Petersen, who purchased the original Cope's press used to make these "curve cuts," as they were sometimes called. The pressed rounds have to be rubbed out, although in the old days, many inventive pipesmokers would simply roll a batch of the rounds up into a cylinder shape and press them into their pipe bowls, breaking off that portion of the tobacco that projected above the pipe. Some of the more forceful smokers simply smashed everything down into the bowl. Since the beginning of the 20th century and continuing to the present day, Escudo is made using only two tobaccos, light Virginia and Perique. It is a thick, sweet and smokey blend, nicely full bodied and perfect for an evening by the fireside or a blustery day on the high seas. HPH 2.5

ESOTERICA — AND SO TO BED — This is another one of those blends you've got to try just because of its name. A medium-length ribbon cut, not stringy and unmanageable, as so many of them are. An elegant, mild English mixture, it has a sweet, subtly smokey aroma and taste. HPH 2

ESOTERICA DUNBAR — Made by G.F. Germain and Son, a small blender in the Channel Island of Jersey, off the coast of England, and primarily sold through American importer and pipemaker Michael Butera. This blend contains seven distinct Virginia tobaccos and just enough Perique to give it real meaning. Thick and spicy sweet, somewhat like a Cavendish without the syrupy thickness. However, I found this ready rubbed tobacco to smoke a bit moist. HPH 2—2.5

FLYING DUTCHMAN — An old time classic tobacco that I remember as a boy. Or perhaps I'm thinking about the book. It doesn't matter. No less than twelve different worldwide tobaccos are used in this aromatic. Finely cut and easy to pack in a pipe, it is not for someone who smokes rapidly, as the tobacco will start to burn hot. Rather, it is for the slow and methodical person who likes a woodsy flavor that is mild but not light. It is a perfect HPH 2.

GERMAIN'S NO. 7 — A mild aromatic blend of Burley and bright Virginia. HPH 1.5—2

GOLD BLOCK — Lightly sweetened with Virginia and spiced with a hint of Burley, this is a very refined and mellow tobacco, perfect for mid-day or late afternoon. I bought my first tin one icy December day in London. Owing to the season, it came wrapped with a special Christmas motif cardboard sleeve (which I think is why I bought it). I remember popping open the tin and smoking a bowlful of Gold Block as I walked along New Bond Street, and how it kept my hands warm in the freezing snow. I think it might have saved my life. HPH 1.5—2

GORDON PYM — A very serious blend of golden yellow Virginia, Maryland, Oriental and dark-fired Virginia tobaccos that is not for the faint of heart. The tin is a bit misleading, for it promises "...a cool and gentle smoke." Cool, maybe yes, but this Latakia-packed blend is about as gentle as a Humvee crashing into a Volkswagen. Make no mistake; this is a slow-burning, full-flavored HPH 2.5—3. Thankfully, the chunky-style beef—-er, leaf— tames its burning rate, so that what you get is a slow, thick, smokey flavor, with just a hint of sweetness at the end of every puff.

HOLGER DANSKE BLACK & BOURBON— Slightly stronger and fuller in body, thanks to its more heavily-flavored casings. HPH 2—2.5

HOLGER DANSKE ORIGINAL HONEY DEW — Blended in Berlin, this is a very light and sweet aromatic, perfect for daytime smoking. HPH 2

HOLLAND HOUSE — A very mild golden Cavendish. HPH 2

INDIAN SUMMER — In addition to the flavors they create, the tobaccos in this medium-strength aromatic were selected because they contain the colorful hues of a forest in the early autumn. Various gold-brown-red grades of flue-cured Virginia, Burley and Oriental tobaccos are used, with a result-ant fruity, sweet and moist favor. Although it is definitely American in image (the package even states the blend is made with some tobaccos that were harvested by the Penn-sylvania Amish), it is very popular in Europe, especially Germany. In fact, I bought one of the very first tins of Indian Summer in the Bremen railroad station over a decade ago. Today it is also available in equally colorful pouches. HPH 2

IWAN RIES THREE STAR BLUE — Although they make a Three Star Grey, Green, Gold, Ebony — and in fact, almost every color and taste in the spectrum — it is the Three Star Blue that has steadfastly remained the leader of the line. At best you could call this a semi-aromatic, as it has some English characteristics. There is a subtle sweetness, not sugary, but more like a honey glaze. The blend exhibits sweet and woodsy herbal flavors, plus a dash of smoke and mint, yet it burns clean and dry. In fact, it is one of the best-burning tobaccos of all those I have tested; one match was all that was needed for a clay bowlful to be smoked right down to the heel (keep this in mind for your next pipesmoking contest). Blended in America by Iwan Ries & Co. in Chicago, the oldest family-owned pipe and cigar store (since 1857) in the country. An altogether refreshing HPH 2.

KENDAL BLACK CHERRY — A decidedly aromatic Cavendish that both smells and subtly tastes like black cher-ries. HPH 2

KENTUCKY BIRD — An extremely mild Danish blend of Tennessee Burley and Golden Virginia and — believe it or not — real dried rose petals. Great for smoking in the garden! It is the perfect springtime smoke, filled with an aromatic fullness of wheat, honey, strawberries and with definite floral undertones. HPH 1.5

LONDON BLEND — A rich, full-bodied concoction of Latakia and Orientals plus Virginia leaf grown in Zimbabwe. Although it is English in taste, it is blended by Timm's in Hamburg, Germany. HPH 2.5

MAC BAREN MIXTURE SCOTTISH BLEND — Heavy, thick and sweet with a great aroma. Full of fire-cured Kentucky, Burley and Virginia tobaccos, this one weighs in with a hefty HPH 2.5 and is the perfect bowlful to light up after a traditional Scottish meal of haggis (finely chopped meat and various animal parts stuffed into a sheep's stomach and cooked), nips (turnips) and tatties (potatoes). Just be sure you have plenty of highland malt whisky to wash it all down.

MAC BAREN VIRGINIA NO. 1 — Extremely light yet with a thick, sweet casing. This is a ready rubbed cake but some smokers may want to rub it out even more to aid combustion and make the tobacco burn a little cooler. HPH 1.5—2

MAC BAREN'S ORIGINAL CHOICE — A rich fruity aroma that is actually stronger than the milder Burly and Virginia blend. The taste is light, lemon-like, and mild. HPH 1.5

MAC BAREN'S PLUMCAKE — Virginia and flue-cured tobaccos produce a blend that is as rich and fruity as the plumcake it is named after. HPH 2—2.5. This is not a tobacco for the meek.

MAC BAREN'S VANILLA CREAM — A new aromatic obviously blended to attract smokers who like dessert, for this blend is like smoking a vanilla cream pie. Blended of loose cut Virginia and black Cavendish, the fresh and delicate cream is intermingled with vanilla in the casing. Yet, for all its richness, the blend is not fattening. HPH 1.5

MALTHOUSE "FOUNDER'S RESERVE" — Virginia tobacco cased with a nondescript single malt, then fermented under pressure for twelve weeks. Noticeably aromatic tasting even though it is not an aromatic per se. Yes, you can taste the Scotch. HPH 2

McCLELLAND BLACK SHAG — First of the 221 B Baker Street series. Thankfully, this is nothing like the original black shag of Holmes' Victorian times, otherwise we'd all be sharing Watson's revulsion to it. Still, I did find enough twigs and mini-boughs in the tin to build a small forest. But once you filter your way down to the deep, rich oily tobacco, you'll find a blend full of enough flavorful spice and nuttiness to satisfy the most ardent sleuth. A medium-strength and thought-inducing smoke, perfect for crime solving or just plain meditating. It is a wonderfully manageable English blend that I first smoked in a blackened clay, but I really think it should be smoked in a calabash. HPH 2.

McCLELLAND BOMBAY COURT — Semi-thick cut Turkish leaf blended with just the right amount of Virginia and Latakia give this medium-strength and slow-burning English mixture a sweet, smokey flavor. It is fashioned somewhat like Dunhill's Durbar, as the blenders tried to match the contents of a 40-year-old tin. So it actually smokes a little like very old Durbar. A must-try for those venturing into the next level of pure English blends. HPH 2

McCLELLAND DOMINICAN GLORY — I had to put this one in for all of the pipemen who are also cigar smokers. This blend was originally conceived to lure cigar smokers to pipes, as the base of this blend consists of mild Dominican cigar leaf. It is a medium light smoke, not altogether unpleasant, but in all fairness, it is more aromatic than most cigars and consequently, doesn't taste exactly like a cigar. That's because the curing of the tobacco is different for cigars than it is for pipes. Rather, it smokes like mild long leaf Piloto Cubano filler tobacco that has been aged with Matured Virginia tobaccos, then pressed, caked, and aged, which is hardly surprising because that's what it is. Although Dominican Glory is ribbon cut to give it the look of an English blend, it actually smokes like a mild aromatic. The caked Virginia emits a sweetness that almost overpowers the cigar leaf, but the smooth spicy Cuban seed taste does manage to ease on through with a medium HPH 2 strength.

McCLELLAND DOMINICAN GLORY MADURO — Now this blend tastes a bit more like a cigar, and kicks in with an HPH 2—2.5. It is the maduro wrapper leaf that makes the difference, which has been blended with red and stoved Virginia tobaccos, then aged, caked and tinned as a very coarse, thick shag which must be rubbed out to fill your pipe. Maduro is a sturdier leaf that has been fermented longer and consequently, has reached a higher temperature in the maturation stage. This, in turn, releases more sugars from the starch in the tobacco leaves. Not surprisingly, this blend smokes sweet, with a more pronounced flavor. The good news for those around you is that both Dominican Glory blends have aromas more akin to pipes than cigars.

McCLELLAND FROG MORTON — A popular English tobacco from one of America's most respected blenders. In fact, this is one of the best of the "new" English tobaccos I have smoked. FrogMorton is a medium rich blend bursting with smokey Latakia and laced with Turkish and some Virginia. An HPH 2.5, it is ideal for long evening walks.

McCLELLAND FROG MORTON GOES TO TOWN — A noticeably lighter version of FrogMorton, easing in at HPH 2. This one is perfect for the all-day smoker who wants a mild yet highly refined Latakia mixture. I used it to break in a new Dunhill five-star that I bought at the Chicagoland Pipe Show and never regretted it.

McCLELLAND NAVY CAVENDISH — For those of you who want to experience what the British Navy was smoking back when they were still being issued daily rations of rum, try a pipeful of this in your clay cutty. Pressed into a traditional cake and seeped for months in Jamaican rum, this hearty leaf is somewhat like battling a pirate ship — it needs to be rubbed out before it can be ignited. The flavor is thick, heavy and sweet, a real swashbuckling smoke. HPH 2.5

McCLELLAND NO. 1 — One of the mildest English tobaccos, made by one of the few (and perhaps best known) blenders in America. A great way to ease into the realm of Latakia. HPH 1.5

McCLELLAND NO. 8 — A very satisfying medium-strength English blend, not overpowering. HPH 2

McCLELLAND NO. 12 — The heaviest English blend in the McClelland line. HPH 2.5—3

MELLOW BREEZE — We're talking Virginia, Oriental and Burley tobaccos sweetened with fruit and vanilla casings. If you like medium HPH 2 aromatics, give this one a try.

MICK McQUAID — A square cut blend that leads me to suspect that ol' Mick was a pretty full-bodied fellow, as this is a pretty full-bodied smoke. HPH 2.5

NAPPA VALLEY — This Danish aromatic blend is light, dry, and fruity and contains a hint of chardonnay. The Nappa name, of course, is inspired by the famous American wine growing region of the Napa Valley (which is actually spelled with one "P") in northern California. The blend is composed of very mild Cavendish, sweet Virginia, and Burley. If you want to smoke a pipe for the first time, this would be an ideal aromatic tobacco with which to launch your venture. HPH 1.5—2

NEPTUNE — Virginia and Burley with a touch of Brazil. Extremely mild and aromatic with a casing of sweet raspberries. HPH 1.5—2

ORLIK CLUB — A relatively new blend designed for smokers who want an extremely mild tobacco. Virginia, Burley and black Cavendish have been lightly top-coated with a delicate fruit flavoring. Frankly, this is as close to an HPH 1 as you are going to get, as it eases in at HPH 1—1.5

ORLIK GOLD MEDAL — Virginia and Oriental tobaccos lightly cased with Jamaican rum produce a medium-strength smoke with a lingering rich aftertaste. Keep your Bacardi 8-Year-Old in the bottle and smoke this instead. HPH 2

PARSONS'S PLEASURE — Appropriately named, this one won't offend anybody. It's as mild as a Sunday afternoon. HPH 1.5—2

PENZANCE — A cross-cut English flake of Virginia, Turkish and Orientals, pressed and cut into thick cakes just waiting to be rubbed out for smoking. HPH 2—2.5

PETER STOKKEBYE EVENING TREASURE — A heavily aromatic blending of black Cavendish with gold and orange Virginia leaf. Sweet and fruity. HPH 2—2.5

PETER STOKKEBYE KENTUCKY NOUGAT — Mild Burleys and Cavendish tobaccos blended with golden African Virginia packed in a loose cut and heavily cased with vanilla flavor accented by a touch of nuts. HPH 2

PETER STOKKEBYE OPTIMUM — Very sweet and fruity and blended with black Cavendish, mild burley, plus flue-cured Zimbabwe and Malawi leaf. HPH 2

PETERSON IRISH OAK — A heavy-bodied dark Cavendish blended with Zimbabwe orange and Thailand Burley leaf. A touch of Perique rounds out this mixture, which is aged in oaken sherry barrels, giving this blend a distinctive sherry taste. A meaty HPH 2.5

PETERSON IRISH WHISKEY — Here is the equivalent of dipping a cigar in brandy. Or in this case, soaking your pipe in whiskey. So now we have a tobacco that enables us to drink and smoke at the same time. Virginia leaf, flue-cured Kentucky, along with Indian and Thailand tobaccos are then blended, aged, and finally misted with Irish whiskey. HPH 2

PETERSON OLD DUBLIN — Introduced in 1998, this is a traditional medium-strength English mixture of Latakia, golden Virginia, black Cavendish and sweet Oriental Basma tobaccos. HPH 2

PETERSON SHERLOCK HOLMES — Another one of those tobaccos you have to buy for the tin, if nothing else. It belongs in every Sherlockian's collection. Besides, how else can you properly smoke your Sherlock Holmes Peterson pipe? An older style straight blend of Virginia leaf, dating back to the gaslight era. HPH 2

PETERSON UNIVERSITY FLAKE — A sliced flake tobacco, so don't even go any further unless you have the time, patience, or curiosity to rub it out by hand before packing it into your pipe. This is a heavy, slow burning smoke, owing to its recipe of various Virginia leaves that have been blended with Indian tobaccos. University flake is appropriately named, for this is indeed the type of tobacco I wish I had when I stayed up all night with just my briar to keep me company as I crammed for finals in college. As a bonus for collectors, it is the most nostalgically attractive tin in the Peterson series of pipe tobaccos. HPH 2.5

PIPE TÜNUNU — A blend that smokes as if it had too much ground pepper mixed in with the nondescript tobacco leaves, which look and taste as if they had been flue-cured in a fireplace full of soot. HPH 2.5

PLAYER'S NAVY CUT — Aromatic and mild. HPH 1.5—2

PUNCHBOWL — A full-bodied English that is bursting with Latakia. This one's like smoking a knockwurst. HPH 2.5—3

R .L. WILL'S SOLANI — From one of Germany's most innovative blenders comes this family of "all natural" blends that consist of the very mild Solani Blue (Virginia, Burley, black Cavendish with a touch of Perique); the slightly spicier Green (red Virginia and double fermented Cavendish), and the meatier red (red Virginia, Orientals, and Latakia). They all fall within the HPH 2 range, with the Solani Red pushing the scale to HPH 2.5

RATTRAY'S ACCOUNTANT'S MIXTURE — A slightly aromatic-behaving English, if you can imagine such a thing. It is slightly sweet with a tart undertaste and smokes a bit moist; you'll need pipe cleaners for this one, which is strictly by the numbers, with an HPH 2.

RATTRAY'S BLACK MALLORY — A full meaty English tobacco with a slight touch of sweetness. If you like a porterhouse steak with a hearty cabernet and then a light custard dessert to top it all off, this is the perfect after-dinner tobacco for you. HPH 2.5

RATTRAY'S MARLIN FLAKE — Similar to Old Gowrie but darker and slightly stronger in flavor and aroma (which you won't smell but those around you will). HPH 2—2.5

RATTRAY'S OLD GOWRIE — A nice, medium flavored Virginia that clocks in at an easy HPH 2.

RATTRAY'S RED RAPPAREE — This famous English tobacco that is now being blended in Germany gets its name from the red Virginia tobaccos that are heavily accented with Oriental leaf. There is a heavy, coarse taste of Latakia with a pleasant sweet and spicy undertaste. Sort of like eating a medium-well steak with a thick Philadelphia char on the outside. HPH 2—2.5

ROYAL VINTAGE GOLDEN CAKE — Flue-cured golden Virginia, aged in cakes to seep in the natural sugars and oils. HPH 1.5—2

ROYAL VINTAGE MATURED VIRGINIA — Three Virginia tobaccos, bright lemon, red, and stoved black, all blended together to produce a medium strength, unobtrusive smoke. HPH 2

SAIL AROMATIC (Green Pouch) — This Dutch Cavendish blend is composed of Oriental and Virginia leaf with mild Burley and strong Latakia playing wonderfully against each other. The result is a very sweet, semi-strong smoke with a very pleasing aroma. HPH 2-2.5

SAMUEL GAWITH CURLY CUT — You're going to have to rub this one out, as you could guess by its name. Flue-cured and steamed light and dark tobaccos have been anointed with vanilla casings, then spun into a tobacco rope and sliced into thin disks. It produces a sweet, semi-mild smoke. HPH 2

SAMUEL GAWITH GROUSE-MOOR — An ancient 200 year old blend that the British were smoking in their clay pipes during the reign of George III. Only three people in the entire Samuel Gawith Company know the ingredients in this mixture. Steamed, flue-cured leaf is aged and then mixed with the "secret ingredients" to produce a medium-strength cacophony of flavors, as firm as a handshake. HPH 2—2.5

SAMUEL GAWITH K.B.E MIXTURE — The initials stand for Kendal Brown English, and those words tell of a long history, starting in 1792, when many of the original Samuel Gawith tobacco recipes were transported by horseback from Scotland to the famed Kendal Brown house in the Lakeland district of Wordsworth fame. A powerhouse HPH 2.5 smoke consisting of 50% Cyprus Latakia and 50% heavily steamed Virginia. Woof!

SAMUEL GAWITH PERFECTION — One of the new British aromatic blends created by Britain's Samuel Gawith & Co. Ltd. to meet the criteria of an anonymous pipesmoker who couldn't seem to find the right blend and finally found it with this tobacco. A mixture of brown and bright Virginia, a dash of Latakia, some vanilla flavoring and the spice of Turkish leaf caused our mysterious pipeman to utter the word which became the blend's name. HPH 2

SAMUEL GAWITH SKIFF MIXTURE — A mild, woodsy-tasting English blend, with a touch of Orientals. Ribbon cut Turkish and black Cyprus Latakia gently carry this one off, just like a sail in the gentle breeze. A good daytime smoke, but for my tastes, a bit too light for the evening. HPH 1.5—2

SAMUEL GAWITH SCOTCH CUT MIXTURE — A hearty English blend of flue-cured tobaccos, including a hint of Latakia and a lacing of black Cavendish. HPH 2.5

SAMUEL GAWITH SQUADRON LEADER — Here's another blend you must smoke just for the name, if nothing else.

Saturday afternoons are best, when the sky is clear, the air is crisp, and the dog is straining at his leash. Ribbon cut Virginia, Latakia and Turkish tobaccos give this blend a spicy lemon and wood aroma and taste. HPH 2

SKANDINAVIK REGULAR CAVENDISH — Burley and Virginia leaf have been given a nut-like flavoring layered over a heavy Cavendish aroma and taste. Thick cut and slow burning. HPH 2

ST. BRUNO — Both flake and ready-rubbed, containing Virginia flue and dark-cured tobaccos, team up to produce a medium HPH 2 strength in this extremely popular blend.

ST. BRUNO READY RUBBED — Here is one of the all-time British greats, although it is no longer being imported into the U.S. Still, in Europe if you can find a can of either the flake or the ready rubbed, and like a rich, full-flavored smoke, give it a try. Virginia flue and dark fire-cured tobaccos create a brisk and flavorful smoke that is perfect for a crisp winter's evening around the hearth. HPH 2.5

STANWELL VANILLA — Introduced in 1998 and mainly available in Germany, this Burley and Virginia Cavendish blend is medium and full flavored with an aroma that smells like someone is baking cookies. HPH 2

THREE NUNS — A classic. Dark-fired and sun cured tobaccos blended with Brazilian leaf; a heady smoke and one of the all-time old favorites. HPH 2—2.5

TORBEN DANSK — A very aromatic blend of Virginia and Latakia. HPH 2—2.5

TROOST — Light flue-cured Virginian and Burley are blended according to a recipe that dates from 1750 to create a very aromatic flavor and aroma with a very satisfying strength of HPH 2. There is also a Troost Special Cavendish blend that utilizes Java tobaccos, has a slight hint of whiskey, and is an HPH 2—2.5

TROOST ULTRA MILD CAVENDISH — I had to put this one in because it is the lightest Cavendish you're likely to smoke. Consequently, it is a great mid-morning blend. A mixture of black Cavendish, brown Virginia Cavendish, and mild bright Virginia, it is extremely slow burning and semi sweet with a slight vanilla taste. HPH 1.5

W.Ø. LARSEN OLD BELT — Ready rubbed, this is a wonderfully sweet ribbon cut honey and lemon-tinged Danish blend with that smokes extremely mild, with a faint nut-like aftertaste. HPH 1.5

W.Ø. LARSEN'S CLASSIC PIPE MIXTURE — One of the most colorful tins around, but more important is what's inside. Assorted fruit with a preponderance of cherries, plus a hint of honey gives a pleasantly mild flavor, with just the tiniest hint of sweetness. This one burns remarkably dry for a cased tobacco. HPH 2

YAYLADAG — A very bland aromatic Turkish tobacco that will leave you a bit giddy and lightheaded. HPH 1—1.5

Some Notes On A Few Of The Alfred Dunhill Hand Blended Tobaccos

Pipesmokers making the pilgrimage to Dunhill's Jermyn Street store in London are sometimes overwhelmed as they ascend the steps to the pipe department on the mezzanine and suddenly find themselves faced with an array of blended tobaccos that are only available in the store. Manager Marc Burrows or one of his able assistants are only too happy to help you sort through the wonderful variety of mixtures, but here is a little advanced information on some of my favorites.

221 B BAKER STREET — I tried this thinking it was an English blend. It wasn't — it was an HPH 2—2.5 aromatic — a clever disguise. Shades of Professor Moriarty!

CHERRY & RUM — I'm including this Alfred Dunhill mixture so all of you aromatic smokers won't think I am prejudiced, which I am, of course. If you take Royal Yacht and add equal amounts of cherry and rum casings, this is what you'll end up with. Smoke it in place of dessert. HPH 2.5

CUBA — MIXTURE 1167 — Yes, this is the one you can't get in America due to the embargo. A wonderful medium strength blend (HPH 2) that smokes slightly sweet with a touch of spice, thanks to the Havana filler leaf and Virginia tobaccos, as well as Orientals and a pinch of Perique. While you may not want to run the risk of trying to sneak a box of Havanas in through U.S. Customs (it is outlawed even for Europeans), a single tin of this tobacco might not draw as much suspicion. Of course, if there are any customs officials reading this book, I'm just kidding. It is a surprisingly mild HPH 2.

DURBAR — One of the greatest of the old Dunhill blends, it has recently been brought back as a tinned tobacco as well. This broad cut mixture of Virginia and Latakia burns extremely slow, which only adds to the enjoyment of the great preponderance of Oriental tobaccos. Its strength fluctuates, depending on how hard a puffer you are, but is within HPH 2—2.5.

JUNE '86 — One of the most popular aromatic tobaccos among pipesmokers from Germany and France. It is a Virginia-based blend lightly cased with Scotch whisky and caramel flavors. HPH 1.5

MIXTURE 27 — Latakia, Oriental, Virginia and Cavendish all work together to produce a medium-mild smoke with a nut-like spicy taste. HPH 2.

MR. ALFRED'S OWN — Also known as Mixture 36080, here is another blend you just must try when visiting Dunhill. It is one of the original Dunhill mixtures and blends Cavendish, Latakia, Virginia and Oriental tobaccos with a touch of Havana to smooth things over. A great HPH 2 mid-afternoon smoke to enjoy as you leave Dunhill and walk down Jermyn Street to Turnbull & Asser to get fitted for a smoking jacket.

WHITE SPOT — You'd have to smoke this, at least once, just for tradition's sake. But be forewarned: it is a very full-bodied HPH 2.5—3 blend of Latakia, Turkish and red Virginia tobaccos. This is a mixture that should be accompanied by a glass of smokey single malt from one of the distilleries on Islay.

Chapter 6

THE PIPESMOKER'S SOURCEBOOK

To help make your pipesmoking even more enjoyable, here are some scattered flakes and dottles of information that you otherwise might not find. Be sure to mention this book when contacting any of these sources.

Pipe Cleaning & Restoration

Sometimes a pipe becomes so charred and clogged it is beyond routine maintenance and needs professional help. Although most tobacconists can handle fundamental pipe rejuvenation such as cleaning and reaming, there are a few experts who can assist in re-staining (being careful not to buff off the original stampings), bit replacement and similar procedures. Try your tobacconist first; if he is unable to perform the required services, have him contact one of the individuals listed below.

Jim Benjamin
12199 Avenida Consentido — Dept. RCH
San Diego, Ca 92128

Jim can take the shoddiest pipe and bring it back to "like new" condition, including bit polishing, rim trimming, and bowl staining to original factory specifications. Simply tell Jim that you want your pipes "Hackerized," which includes cleaning and reaming, but no re-staining, a very light waxing, and absolutely no buffing around any of the stamped nomenclature on either the bit or the briar. In fact, nothing more abrasive than a butterfly's eyelash should ever touch the stamping. But Jim knows that.

Rich Lewis
Lewis Pipe & Tobacco
512 Nicollet Avenue — Dept. RCH
Minneapolis, MN 55402

A pipemaker himself, Rich does factory repairs for Ashton, Ser Jacopo, Radice, Ferndown, Upshall and selected other brands as well as meerschaums. He can also hand cut replacement bits from solid vulcanite.

> Mr. Paul's Pipe Repair
> P.O. Box 47145 — Dept. RCH
> Baltimore, MD 21244-7145

Thirty-five years of pipe repairs and cleaning have given Mr. Paul the experience to repair everything from cracked shanks to burned out bowls. Send for his complete list or seek him out on the internet.

Antique Accessories
Dixie Gun Works
Gunpowder Lane
Union City, TN 38261

Clay pipes, early American tobacco and snuff boxes; flint and steel fire starters and reproduction tinder lighters. Send $5 for their phone book-sized catalog, that is also full of 18th and 19th century rifles, clothing and related paraphernalia.

Publications for Pipesmokers
International
PIPE Magazine
Postbus 3022
2480 AA Woubrugge
The Netherlands

Published by Rothmans International Tobacco Products, this international publication is printed in four languages — English, French, German and Spanish — and sent to tobacconists around the world twice a year for distribution to their customers. The wide variety of articles on pipes and related lifestyle activities make this colorful publication well worth reading from cover to cover. You may even find an article or two by the author of this book. If you want the magazine to come directly to your home, the annual subscription is a mere $10, well worth it for the wealth of information within its pages.

> The Pipe Year Book
> c/o Académie Internationale de la Pipe
> 1, Avenue Robert Schuman
> 75347 Paris
> France

A thick softcover book published annually by the Académie Internationale de la Pipe and containing articles in English, French, and German. The material, which is extremely well researched and borders on the scholastic, is written by Académie members, which means you may occasionally find a few of the author's articles, as my schedule permits.

Austria

CIGAR CULT JOURNAL
Dr. Helmet Romé/Hans Dibol
Falstaff-Verlag
Büropark Donau
Inkustrasse 1-7/Stg. 4/2 OG
A-3400 Klosterneuburg

In spite of its name, pipes play an important editorial and pictorial part in this slick, thick colorful lifestyle magazine. What makes it especially appealing is the fact that many of the articles are printed in English as well as German.

Czech Republic

CIGAR & COCKTAIL
P.O. Box 61
150 21 Prague 5

A thick, glossy, colorful magazine that started in the spring of 1999 and centers on the lifestyle of the pipe and cigar smoker in the Eastern block of Europe.

Denmark

PIBER & TOBAK
Leif Slot, Editor
Ellekrattet 18
2950 Vedbaek

A colorful journal on pipesmoking, made even more colorful if you happen to read Danish. Even so, the photographs of products and events are fascinating.

England

THE PIPEMAN MAGAZINE
Hendon Road
Sunderland SR9 9XZ

Published quarterly by the Imperial Tobacco Company. A great colorful lifestyle read for any pipeman, British or otherwise. However, Britain's prejudiced anti-smoking laws may spell the end of this enjoyable magazine, so check to see if it is readily available, or if free speech has ceased to exist.

France
REVUE DES TABACS
16, rue Saint-Fiacre
75002 Paris
Michel Burton's bimonthly publication with beautiful color covers and much news of the world situation as it pertains to tobacco. In addition to the magazine, a highly informative quarterly newsletter is also published.

Germany
PIPE & CIGAR
Ebner Verlag
Karlstrasse 41
D-89073 Ulm (Donau)
Under the editorial guidance of editor Frank Hidien, this wonderful publication is a fascinating, thick, colorful smoker's magazine devoted to pipes, cigars, clubs, fashions, drink, and all those great elements that make the pipesmoking lifestyle so enjoyable.

SMOKER'S CLUB
(formerly known as Pipe Club)
Postfach 3120
55021 Mainz
Lots of color photographs and interesting articles about pipes, pipesmoking and pipemakers.

DIE TABAK ZIETUNG
P. O. Box 3120
D-6500 Mainz 1

Italy
AMICI DELLA PIPA
Casella Postale 10734
Roma
A publication with much news, photography and advertisements concerning pipes and pipemakers, still being published by enthusiastic pipeman-editor Giancarlo Fortunado.

SMOKING
Via della Farnesina, 224
00194 Roma
Published by Fausto Fincato, proprietor of Rome's famed Fincato pipe shop, which has been attracting pipesmokers since 1932. SMOKING is a superbly produced four-color maga-

zine with photographs that make you want to light a pipe whenever you flip through the pages. The excellent graphics make SMOKING worth having even if you don't read Italian. For a while the magazine had ceased publication but now it is back, this time adding cigars to its formerly pipes-only pages.

Poland

Janusz Terakowski, Editor
KALUMET
Box 758
30-960 Krakow 1

I don't read Polish so I have no idea what the articles are about, but this magazine has pipes in it, and that's good enough for me.

United States of America

PIPES AND TOBACCO
3000 Highwoods Blvd., Suite 300
Raleigh, NC 27604-1029

A quarterly magazine that is colorful and full of articles on tobacco, pipes, pipemakers, products, personalities, clubs and events.

PIPE FRIENDLY
P.O. Box 13781 — Dept. RCH
Torrance, CA 90503

A quarterly black and white magazine put out by Joel Farr. Product reviews and American club news is included, along with articles that primarily represent a forum for the magazine's subscribers. This obvious labor of love by the publisher is worth subscribing to, if for nothing else than the written commentary by many of its readers. Write for current subscription rate.

THE PIPE SMOKER'S EPHEMERIS
20-37 120th Street — Dept. RCH
College Point, NY 11356

The original international newsletter of casual, relaxing informative reading for pipesmokers, published for over 30 years by Tom Dunn, one of pipesmoking's most enthusiastic boosters. This thick "irregular quarterly" comes out once or twice a year and is eagerly awaited by a worldwide audience of readers interested in pipes, cigars, lighters, tobacco, Sherlock Holmes and virtually anything else even remotely connected with pipes and smoking. Subscriptions are free but do Tom a favor and send a donation of money, postage stamps, pipes or a sample of your favorite tobacco.

Miscellaneous Organizations

Frankly, there are just too many pipe clubs to put in a book of this size. Best bet is to get on the internet and check them all out at *http://www.pipes.org*. That's where you'll find Steve Masticola's universal cyberworld linkups to practically every pipe-related web page on this planet.

In addition, you'll find numerous clubs listed in Tom Dunn's Pipe Smoker's Ephemeris. However, there is one club that you may not find, so here it is:

> Pipe Able
> 1359 Keoncrest Avenue — Dept. RCH
> San Jose, CA 95110
> *www.pipeable.org*

The creation of Charles Beeson, this is an organization for physically challenged men and women who are taught how to use a pipe to relax and cope with stress. A victim of MS, Chuck practices what he preaches and is now helping others to do the same. Be sure to inquire about Pipe Able's limited edition Sherlock Holmes humidor, pictured elsewhere in this book.

Additional Readings/Reference Works

Pipes and books seem to go together, so here are some of my favorite volumes that may help your next bowlful smoke just a little more enjoyable than before.

Barrie, J. M. *My Lady Nicotine*. London: Hodder and Stoughton, 1890.

Dunhill, Alfred. *The Pipe Book*. London: A. & C. Black, Ltd. New York: The MacMillan Co., 1924; revised ed., London: Arthur Barker Limited; New York: The MacMillan Co., 1969., New York: The Lyons Press, 1999.

Dunhill, Alfred H. *The Gentle Art of Smoking*. London: Max Reinhardt Ltd.; New York: G.P. Putnam and Sons, 1954.

Dunhill, Mary. *Our Family Business*. London: The Bodley Head; 1979.

Ehwa, Carl Jr. *The Book of Pipes and Tobacco*. New York: Random House, 1974.

Herment, Georges. *The Pipe*. New York: Simon and Schuster, 1955.

Pollner, Otto. *Die Pfeifenmacher*. Heka-Verlag, 1997.

Whifflets. Compiled by A. M. Jenkinson. Pittsburgh: R. & W. Jenkinson Co., 1897.

> *Tobacco Encyclopedia*
> Tobak-Journal International
> Postfach 3120
> 6500 Mainz am Rhein—Germany

Published in 1984, this is a collection of more than 6,000 tobacco terms and their meanings. In English.

WANT TO LEARN MORE?

Read These Other Smoking-Hot Books by Richard Carleton Hacker

RARE SMOKE
The Ultimate Guide
To Pipe Collecting

• The first book devoted to 20th century estate pipes

• Limited edition — only 2,500 copies — a book destined to become as collectable as the pipes it describes

• Hundreds of exclusive *facts* on Dunhill, Barling, Charatan, Sasieni, Peterson, Comoy's, GBD, Castello, Kaywoodie, Demuth, Custombilt, Marxman and *more*!

• The only *authenticated* Dunhill dating guide.

• Chapters on Christmas and Limited Edition pipes

• Collector's Compendium of every pipe brand in the world

• Pipe values • Counterfeits • Buying on and off the internet

• Pipe Collector's Sourcebook

Only $37.50

Hardcover • 288 pages
Over 165 black & white and color photos

...Then See The Movie!

The Ultimate PIPE VIDEO

The Sights & Sounds of Pipesmoking

- The pipe lighting ritual
- Interviews with pipemakers
- Pipe buying in *real-time action*
- Tobacco blending
- Pipemaking
- MPV — the world's first Pipe Musical Video

Only $34.95

60 Minutes (approx. 1.5 pipefuls) VHS (U.S. format only)
Available at the very *best* tobacconists!

For more information contact:

P.O. Box 634 • Beverly Hills, CA 90213 • USA